THREE AND A TREE

160over90
Philadelphia, Pennsylvania, 2012

Published by:
One Sixty Over Ninety, Inc.
1 South Broad Street, 10th Floor
Philadelphia, PA 19107

Written & Designed by: 160over90

Table of Contents

Foreword
By: Mireille Grangenois
Publisher, The Chronicle of Higher Education

Marketing is truth and beauty.

This was the first and most important lesson I received immediately after being named Vice-President of Marketing at *The Baltimore Sun*. Many years later, now as Publisher of *The Chronicle of Higher Education* and *The Chronicle of Philanthropy*, I still adhere to this tenet.

If you too appreciate this wisdom and seek to practice it, or don't even know what it means, "Three And A Tree" is a smart, accessible, and oft-times irreverent guide to the under-examined world of higher ed marketing.

While university marketing is not always well executed or understood, even at times among campus administrators responsible for it, we all are inundated by it. Try escaping the bombardment of collegiate marketing sameness while walking through an airport, driving past billboards on a major highway, or gazing at the side of public buses in any city.

No one is better poised to de-construct, critique and demystify the college marketing process than the agency 160over90. Having worked with institutions of all types, sizes, and standings, 160over90 is helping higher ed leaders discover how to uniquely express their missions, and breathe new life into brands that were generic, flaccid, and lacking distinction.

"A brand is a perception, and that perception is shaped by every single experience (touchpoint) a person has with your organization," 160over90 writes. "A brand is a story...And it has to ring true."

With equal parts wit, clarity, and genius, 160over90 shares insights into the process that helps uncover an institution's essence – its brand's story. 160over90 then finds the most original and creative expression for that story – its "truth and beauty."

I first learned of 160over90 from articles written in *The Chronicle* in 2007 and again in 2010 on the agency's work with Wilkes University. In both instances, I was struck by their arresting interpretation of what "personal attention to the student" – Wilkes' essential truth – could look and feel like to a potential and an actual incoming student.

And that leads to my next point: College marketing covers a broad landscape. In this book, 160over90 is particularly focused on those efforts aimed at high school students whom colleges and universities want to recruit. While the demographic profiles of enrolled college students range from working adults, returning veterans, and online learners of all ages, there is a huge, renewable population of teens available to embrace or reject the marketing of your institution's brand every year.

Here, 160over90 fairly shines. The book confronts the uncomfortable realities and dysfunctions of marketing at many higher ed institutions: the absence of marketing literacy, the fragmented budgets, the widely dispersed responsibility for branding, pervasive cynicism, and the many disconnects from a brand with the lived experience.

The book allows readers to nod in violent agreement as it critiques myriad examples of a rampant condition – TAAT for "Three And A Tree" – that anyone who has ever looked at a student recruiting brochure has surely been exposed to.

But 160over90 pushes well beyond that critique to provide a conceptual roadmap for getting your marketing house in order, and along the way, offers high level guidance usually reserved for paying clients. I should know.

I am one! As I write this, both *Chronicles* are engaged with 160over90 for our own branding efforts.

160over90 learned higher ed marketing by trial and error and by translating what they already culled from their consumer marketing work aimed at youths. If you are responsible for messages targeting college-bound high school students, it is most intuitive to gain insights from an agency with clients like Nike and American Eagle Outfitters and apply its knowledge to your student recruiting challenges.

Candid, insightful, and fresh, "Three and A Tree" stirs its readers to shake off crowd-sourced clichés and regimented approaches.

Whether you come away inspired to lead your own internal marketing team and institutional stakeholders or retain the help of 160over90 or another agency to tackle your marketing challenges, after reading this book, you will be better equipped.

And I promise you will never look at yours or any other college's student recruitment brochure the same way.

Yours in truth and beauty,

Mireille Grangenois

Washington, D.C.

July 2012

INTRODUCTION

Do you suffer
from TAAT?

Here's a simple test to find out if you suffer from TAAT. Gather your school's marketing materials, and spread them out wide on a table in front of you. There it is, right there, on the cover of your viewbook: Three And A Tree. Three students of varying ethnicities and gender, dressed head-to-toe in college-branded merchandise. One student has a backpack slung oh-so-casually over the shoulder. He must be on his way to class. The other two are perched over a laptop. (Say, I bet they're on the campus WiFi!) All three are grinning from ear-to-ear, as if they just shared a lighthearted anecdote about the mechanical engineering textbook sitting open on the lawn. Or maybe they're all looking at the camera, beckoning you to join them under the majestic elm tree on the stately university quad.

In extreme cases, you may experience TAATPTDPF: Three And A Tree Plus Two Dudes Playing Frisbee.

For far, far too long, higher ed marketing has been rife with clichés like TAAT. Seriously, spread out your marketing materials in front of you. We'll wait. After all, that's exactly what some high school students do when they get home from a grueling day at a college fair. They haul one, maybe two complimentary Kaplan Test Prep-branded plastic bags bursting with brochures up to their bedroom, dump them out on their beds, and let their eyes roam to whatever covers grab their attention. Even then, they don't pick up each brochure and dutifully start reading at the top of page one. Some start at the back. Others thumb through them like a flip book, maybe pausing to read something here or there. Each brochure has milliseconds to make an impression, and those that fail find their way to the circular file. If you've relied on clichés like Three And A Tree and their ilk, your viewbook might already be in said trash bin.

But let's assume you got lucky. Maybe you did everything right, and now you're on the student's short list. The student's next stop is likely your website, where he or she is forced to wade through news articles about your new graduate program, a form where the student can search the library holdings, a notice about a snow closure, meal plans, and 60+ other links on the home page, just to get to the information they're interested in.

Joy of joys, they actually signed up to attend an open house and campus tour. The one that starts in the basement cafeteria with the boarded up windows (true story). The one led by the kid who enjoys pointing out which dorm is easiest to sneak beer into (again, true). The kid you're relying upon to convince high schoolers and their nervous parents that they should write $120,000 in checks to you over the next four years.

That viewbook, your website, and that overzealous kid are all major touch points of your brand. Ah, there's that word: brand. When many people hear it, they immediately think logo, tagline, or a television ad. But to us, a brand is so much more. It's a perception, a perception shaped by every single experience someone has with your organization. A brand is a story, with a great hook at the beginning, a lot of meat in the middle, and a solid ending that makes the whole journey worthwhile. And it has to ring true. We're 160over90, a branding agency with offices in Philly and Newport Beach, CA, founded by business partners Shannon Slusher and Darryl Cilli. It's our agency's job to help organizations of all stripes tell their stories in compelling and surprising ways.

We started developing university brands almost by accident. We were just a couple of years into our existence in 2002 when Chestnut Hill College—a small, suburban, female-only school—came knocking. Like many single-sex institutions, it was struggling mightily with enrollment. In fact, "struggling" is an understatement. With each passing class, numbers were dwindling, and the tiny college was on the brink of extinction.

Chestnut Hill asked our fledgling agency—with zero higher education branding experience—to help them go co-ed. We were a risky bet. We had a fair amount of consumer marketing under our belts, specifically working with brands that catered to the youth market, and Chestnut Hill hoped we could bring just a few of those insights to their school to help them perform a complete turn-around. The school's very existence was on the line, and we had to not just market the school, but market it to both sexes. Not an easy task when not a single male had yet set foot in a classroom.

So we started with a viewbook, a small, humble guide to what the student experience would look like in the fall of 2003, when (we hoped) the student body would have just a little more testosterone.

Before embarking on the project, we had a few of our interns pose as high school students and had them sign up for a bunch of Chestnut Hill's competitors' marketing materials. The brochures soon began pouring in. And they were embarrassingly dull. It was as if the last 20 years of consumer, branding, design, and marketing had passed higher ed by, and it soon became clear that schools were seemingly relying on the materials from other schools for their inspiration—a vicious circle resulting in lazy design, bored copywriting, and tired photography. Each brochure we received felt like a halfhearted copy of the last.

We knew to help save Chestnut Hill, we had to kick their brand so far away from other higher ed marketing that it couldn't help but stand on its own and get attention. We used everything we had learned in consumer marketing to find out what made Chestnut Hill unique, then discover meaningful, relevant ways to tell that story to 17-year-olds and their parents. We set a team of copywriters to work on carefully constructing every word and writing headlines for sections of the view-book that were just a touch more engaging than typical headers like "Academic Opportunities" and "Student Life." For photography, we hired respected fashion, architecture, and still life photographers to cast a whole new light on the Chestnut Hill campus. And our designers looked to the campus itself for inspiration, drawing upon architectural elements of the buildings and classrooms to form the basis of how all our materials looked—influencing everything from the typefaces we selected to the grid we used for our layouts. Finally, we wrapped the whole brochure in a stark, cream-colored book jacket that had the texture of a fine, linen paper lined with a fleur-de-lis pattern that lent the book the appearance of having the lining of an Ivy League-esque sport coat—hopefully sending the message that this school was worth considering, since they took the time to actually care what they were sending to you. Held in the hand, the book felt like a little, considered gift from your friends at Chestnut Hill. One that was an honest, true reflection of the institution and its educational philosophy.

We then embarked on overhauling every other interaction a high school student would have with the brand. We restructured, redesigned, rewrote, and rebuilt the website. We designed a new admissions lobby. The gryphon mascot got a facelift. And what do you know, it all started to work. By 2005, enrollment increased 80 percent. We were now working with the school's admission staff to help develop strategies, marketing plans, and every piece of marketing the school sent out.

Chestnut Hill College was thrilled, and so were we, with a great case study that soon drew the attention of other area schools.

Fast forward to 2012, and 160over90 has now worked with more than 35 schools nationwide, Catholic and secular, public and private, from 1,000 students to 50,000—including Michigan State University, the University of Notre Dame, UCLA, and MIT. We've evolved our skills to brand not just undergraduate recruitment efforts, but entire universities, shaping brands that reach every audience at every point of contact.

Along the way, we've also maintained a healthy roster of non-higher ed clientele, including Nike, Mercedes-Benz, American Eagle Outfitters, the Miami Dolphins, and others. The lessons we've learned on consumer brands like these have informed the work of our higher ed clients, and vice versa. At 160over90, we now consider ourselves in a unique position to be a pretty damn fine branding agency that also happens to have a solid handle on how to market higher ed. And Chestnut Hill College is still a client of ours 10 years later.

But we've also made a lot of mistakes along the way—and yes, we even found ourselves guilty of relying on Three And A Tree on at least one early occasion. Which brings us to this book.

We wrote this book not as a higher ed branding bible, or an academic treatise on the state of university marketing, but as a sort of diary of some of the things we've learned along the way to help schools in some cases double their applications, and where we've failed miserably—like the time we created an environmentally friendly paperless communications cycle that got a whopping zero-percent response from prospective students. This book is also a collection of what we consider our fundamental truths of what we think it takes to brand a school, and how you can work to eliminate clichés in your materials so that they get results.

This book won't make you a better marketer, designer, or writer. It won't tell you exactly what you should do for your university—it's not an all-encompassing, step-by-step guide. These are simply our insights and beliefs that we think can help steer you to more successful, efficient, and effective branding.

It's written essentially in three parts. The first section discusses how we define the term "branding," and what it means in a higher ed context.

The second tells how to jump start a branding program, build a branding team within your college or university, how to hire some help, and how to put a process in place so you don't flail around and hurt someone.

Finally, we talk about what it takes to actually roll your brand out to your audiences (hint: internally first, then externally) in the most creative, compelling, memorable, and lasting way possible. Get it right, and you can see your institution's reputation take leaps and bounds. Mess up here—as some major universities have recently by keeping their efforts a secret until the last possible moment—and you'll have students, faculty, and alumni asking for your head on a platter.

The last thing we'll add is that while we hope you find this book to be in some way useful, we're not going to pretend that this is anything but a sales piece (and a thinly veiled one at that) hawking our services. If you've read this book and think we might be a good fit for your organization, or if you'd just like to share your thoughts, please get in touch at contact@160over90.com.

You can also follow us on Facebook and at @160over90 on Twitter.

Sincerely,
The staff at ONESIXTYOVERNINETY

1

GETTING TO KNOW YOU,

BRANDING

"Look,
you simply can't
sum us up with a
soundbite."

So begins at least one conversation between a university and their marketing/advertising/branding agency. It might come from a disgruntled tenured professor in the humanities department with a dull axe to grind. Might even come from the president (who may be equally gruntled). At some point, someone will come to a meeting loaded for bear, ready to take down the fancy big-city branding firm who thinks they know it all. We even once endured a member of an executive board who asked that we strike the word "branding" from our contract. They're skeptical. They look at agencies as if they're riding into town in top hats, ready to sell folks on some snake oil. Branding is a four-letter word, and those who choose this line of work should be prepared to line up behind personal injury lawyers and the guy who sells you on the undercarriage treatment as Those-Who-Cannot-Be-Trusted.

All we ask, then, is that you hear us out while we offer our perspective on what branding is, and what it isn't.

Branding has been around since cavemen were scrawling on walls with pictograms telling other tribes "these people hunt" or "good fishing here" or "hungry dinosaur cave, best keep out." (We know, there were several eons between humans and the stegosaurus, but go with us here.) Whenever people needed to create an impression, tell a story, or change a perception, they were really branding. Egyptians had pyramids that told the world "a great king is buried here." Early Christians had disciples, crusaders, an early version of a viewbook (if you pardon the metaphor) that summed up their beliefs, and a symbol for all the world to turn to— the cross. Cattle herders help dissuade rustlers and mark their quality livestock with a quite literal brand burned into the hides of their animals. The Redcoats of the British army—in all their military finery—sent a message to the ragtag colony rebels that theirs was an imperial force to be reckoned with, which, fortunately for us, made for easy pickins in dense Appalachian forests.

Fast forward to the 20th century, when businesses (and eventually corporations) with antacids, sports cars, sugar water, life insurance, and hamburgers to sell learned that they needed to find a way to not only make the public aware of their products, but also tell people why they were different from every other stand selling five-cent burgers on the newly blacktopped interstates. They needed to build a case why their product was better, and get that message to stick in a way that they became a person's regular choice whenever they were hungry. And so modern-day branding was born.

Put simply, a brand is a perception. It may be positive or negative, skin-deep or nearly bottomless. It's a narrative or story about your organization that exists in the minds of all of your various audiences, and those audiences are very likely to not all carry the same perception. Advertising, marketing, branding, design (or whatever you want to call them) firms very rarely create these perceptions outright, but they do help shape them. When an organization is known to have a weak brand, it doesn't mean it's wrong, the "weakness" refers to the fact that if you speak to a group of individuals about what your organization stands for, you're likely to get some wildly different answers. On the other hand, an organization with a strong brand is adept at shaping its perception in such a way that all the stars align and the people you want to care about you and your product are saying very similar things about who you are. Great brands are an ongoing narrative—truthful, honest reflections of who the organization really is, and great brands reflect the aspirations for where the organization is heading.

Ask a handful of people with at least a rudimentary understanding of branding what they think the most powerful brand is today, and you'll quickly hear "Apple." Why? It's not just because Apple makes some pretty amazing hardware. You can feel there's a corporate ethos at play behind the company. Its website backs up that experience. Its package design and minimalist instruction manuals back up purchase decisions (and lead to a trend of "unboxing" videos online, giving jealous voyeurs a virtual Christmas-morning experience). Apple's stores, complete with a personal appointment-only Genius Bar, invite the public to check out new products in a stately museum-like atmosphere. Product leaks get more press then celebrity rehab stints. When Steve Jobs walked out on a stage, you'd know exactly what he was going to be wearing: faded Levi's jeans and an Issaye Miyake black mock turtleneck. Head preacher in the Cult of Apple.

All of these examples do such a phenomenal job of branding Apple that when you talk to people about what Apple represents, you'll hear the same things over and over: sleek, easy-to-use, minimalist, helpful, clean, premium. And that's exactly the perception Jobs—and his longtime ad agency TBWA/Chiat/Day—wanted you to have. You couldn't ask for a stronger brand. Still, there are those with negative perceptions about the company: expensive, elitist, protective. These people aren't wrong, they just have a different point-of-view. Apple could have spent even more money trying to preach to the non-converted, but in the end Jobs seemed happy with the following in the congregation.

So what of colleges and universities? Where does branding fit in? You have to start with the competition. It seems that from about the early 19th century until, oh, about the dawn of WWII, anyone with a personal philosophy and a bankroll decided to start a college. And a fair number of them (let's settle on the U.S. Department of Education's 2008 number of 6,551), have survived to the present day. The competition is massive— locally, nationally, and now, internationally. Your audience is, most likely, just about everyone. Current students. Alumni (old, young, rich, and student-loan poor). The local community. Adult learners. Graduate students. Senators. Congress. Corporations. Anyone holding the key to a research grant. Internal faculty. Faculty you're trying to recruit. Sports fans. Oh, not to mention high school students, their parents, and guidance counselors. It seems like the only individuals not being communicated to are babies and dogs—and more than a few schools are already selling apparel to them too.

In the face of all this competition and all these audiences, schools need to do three things flawlessly to stand out:

—————————————— 1 ——————————————

**Figure out who they are today and what
they want to accomplish in the future.**

—————————————— 2 ——————————————

**Discover and cultivate the truly unique
characteristics that can help them reach these goals.**

—————————————— 3 ——————————————

**Find the most efficient, consistently meaningful
methods to communicate these differences to
each audience at every opportunity.**

If only it were that simple. You can't have steps 2 and 3 without executing 1 successfully. And you can have 1 and 2 down pat, but fall flat on your face when it comes to number 3. Worst of all, the vast majority of schools struggle significantly with all three. Let's spend some time breaking down each step.

A school's broad-based goals need to be defined by an executive board, in the form of mission and vision statements and strategic plans. A perfect starting point, if your organization can reach a consensus on what these goals are. More than a few have fallen short in this area, making the second two objectives all the more difficult. But when the strategic plan is locked down and accepted, the door is open for branding to come in and make some headway.

With a strong strategic plan in place, you can begin working with an agency on your research phase, beginning with a series of interviews with as many people as possible. Those interviews usually include the President, Provost, all the top VPs, executives and directors, key alums, students (current and prospective), and deans and faculty in every department—even students who ultimately decided to enroll elsewhere. We've also been known to talk to everyone from the university archivist and the guy who drives the school's shuttle bus after Saturday night fraternity parties. Agencies do all this to learn one thing: What really makes you distinctive?

Truth be told, it's not an easy task. Agencies are often informed of what these "unique" factors are on Day One of an engagement by a well-meaning representative of the school, and they usually include one, some, or several (ugh) of the following. Stop us if you've heard these before:

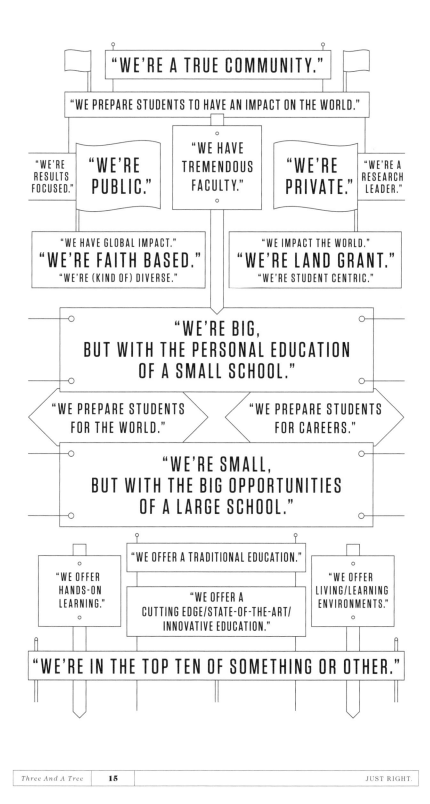

"WE'RE A TRUE COMMUNITY."

"WE PREPARE STUDENTS TO HAVE AN IMPACT ON THE WORLD."

"WE'RE RESULTS FOCUSED."

"WE'RE PUBLIC."

"WE HAVE TREMENDOUS FACULTY."

"WE'RE PRIVATE."

"WE'RE A RESEARCH LEADER."

"WE HAVE GLOBAL IMPACT."
"WE'RE FAITH BASED."
"WE'RE (KIND OF) DIVERSE."

"WE IMPACT THE WORLD."
"WE'RE LAND GRANT."
"WE'RE STUDENT CENTRIC."

"WE'RE BIG,
BUT WITH THE PERSONAL EDUCATION
OF A SMALL SCHOOL."

"WE PREPARE STUDENTS
FOR THE WORLD."

"WE PREPARE STUDENTS
FOR CAREERS."

"WE'RE SMALL,
BUT WITH THE BIG OPPORTUNITIES
OF A LARGE SCHOOL."

"WE OFFER A TRADITIONAL EDUCATION."

"WE OFFER
HANDS-ON
LEARNING."

"WE OFFER A
CUTTING EDGE/STATE-OF-THE-ART/
INNOVATIVE EDUCATION."

"WE OFFER
LIVING/LEARNING
ENVIRONMENTS."

"WE'RE IN THE TOP TEN OF SOMETHING OR OTHER."

The list goes on, but you probably get the point. Everyone has something they think they excel at, but the reality is that you're rarely number one at what you do, and it's highly likely that you're telling people the same thing that one of your direct competitors is saying—and they're probably saying it better without as much jargon. Good luck getting any of these messages to stick.

The lesson here is that very few organizations are truly unique. It's your job to find out what makes you the most different, then find a unique way to tell that story. That's why branding firms often conduct discovery interviews. You may hear from twenty people about how a school is "focused on students." But it's all hot air until a student tells you a story about how his engineering professor invited him to his home for dinner to discuss a possible move to another major, based on the professor's observations that the student's potential could have greater impact in another program. It's stories like these that can only come from conversations, and they're the proof that an organization can really live up to its promises. These essential truths are what great brands are based on. An example often cited is the early decades of MTV, back when they actually aired music videos. They never tried to sell people on the fact they were "cool," they just were. People felt it. And that Guns N' Roses "November Rain" video was proof positive. If they came out and tried to tell people they were something else, it wouldn't ring true. It would still be snake oil, just in a bottle hawked by Pat Benatar and Billy Idol.

Jumping back to that Apple example from earlier (we wish we didn't have to rely on Apple so often for examples, they're just so good), one of our creative directors said he always understood what Apple stood for, but it was all made whole one morning on a visit to the Chicago Apple Store on Michigan Ave., where he was greeted by an employee giving product demos—who also happened to be blind. This creative director was so taken by the fact that one of its employees, charged with demonstrating simplicity to hundreds of customers every day, was without sight, that it made everything about the Apple experience gel for him. It's moments like these that are what we refer to as "Brand Touchpoints," and there's another branding lesson to be learned here.

A brand is not a logo, a tagline, a television ad, or a brochure. As we said before, a brand is a perception, and that perception is shaped by every single experience (touchpoint) a person has with your organization. A brand is a story, with a great hook at the beginning, a lot of meat in the middle, and a solid ending that makes the whole journey worthwhile. And it has to ring true. You may have outright spit-on-the-ground hatred of the term "brand," but you already have one—whether you like it or not. The best brands recognize this.

Let's walk through a typical brand experience a high school student may have with a college:

Madison is a B-average, 16-year-old junior at a public high school. She's not really focused on college, other than the fact that she knows she should probably go to one. She doesn't quite know or understand how she's going to pay for it either, but hopes things will work out when the time comes. She's heard of some of the prestigious schools, can name a few of the big schools in her state, and knows about a small university in another state because she has a cousin who goes there.

Because she's a junior, she's starting to get these brochures and postcards from a bunch of places she may or may not have heard of. She thumbs through a few, and they're filled with pictures of what a "good" school looks like. Smiling kids. Lots of trees and flowers. Old-looking buildings. But after a while they all start to look the same, and before long, these brochures are only getting a cursory glance before finding their way to the trash.

As she enters the summer of her junior year, the bundles of mail are getting a little thicker. She's beginning to feel the pressure from her parents and guidance counselor, and she sees her friends going on campus tours. She doesn't have an inkling about what she wants as a career six years from now, but maybe she wants to be a veterinarian, or a news anchor, or a teacher, or maybe a fashion designer. Her family is also pressuring her to be a doctor or study law. They buy her a few of the fat "Guide to America's Best Colleges" books from the local Barnes and Noble, then sit down together to make a list of schools worth visiting. She spends a couple of minutes visiting each school's website, and immediately crosses a few names off her list because they "look boring." A few, though, leave an impression, so she fills out a form for a campus tour. Her public state school's site, in particular, hits the mark because it was really easy to schedule a tour, and someone from the school even called her later to ask her if she had any questions about her visit before she arrives.

She goes on the tours she picked, and is dragged to two others by her constantly hovering parents. One school has a really ugly campus and a quiet tour guide who doesn't seem to know much about the buildings, other than where the gym is and what food is available at the cafeteria. At another, she's overwhelmed by a crowded admissions dungeon jammed with other nervous kids. At a third, her parents struggle to find a place to park after being turned away by an aggressive parking attendant, and was offered a self-guided tour after learning that her name was mistakenly left off the tour schedule.

At State, however, everything seemed great. Even though it was summer, there were a lot of students walking around. A few held doors for them as they walked around the gorgeous campus. The tour guide was really funny and knew his stuff, and they served an awesome taco salad in the cafeteria (free for prospective students). Yes, they offer a veterinary and a pre-law program, but no fashion design. And a person from admissions greeted her and her parents by name and even gave her a really cool T-shirt, printed on American Apparel no less.

State gains big points in her book, and moves to the top of her list. That fall, back at high school, someone from State visits the school, and despite his combover, he makes a pretty good case about how State is about "a community based around you," which is something she heard and felt when she was on campus. She also learns two of her friends on lacrosse are applying there, but is warned off of the school by her cousin, who transferred out of State after a semester, and a co-worker of her mother's who said it's a "diploma factory," whatever that is. Still, she can really see herself living there, and the commercial she saw at halftime during one of State's nationally televised games didn't completely suck, so she and her parents decide that State's going to be her first choice, even if State requires an essay about "what community means to you" on its application. Hopefully, the financial aid works out too.

All hypothetical, sure, but probably pretty true based on conversations we have all the time with kids. It hopefully offers a little insight into all the touchpoints that shape Madison's brand perception about a school. Yes, she probably saw a logo and glanced at a couple of brochures. She spent a few minutes on the website. But her impression may have also been shaped by a tour guide, a phone call, a TV commercial, a conversation with a classmate or a cousin, or one of a thousand other interactions she had along the way.

Make no mistake, any school that depends upon tuition for the lion's share of its revenue should set delivering the particular education it promises to students as its primary goal. But secondarily, proving that you deliver the goods to anyone who comes in contact with your organization is a close second. The stories you tell and prove at every single touchpoint shape the perception of your school. If the stories are not consistent, meaningful, memorable, and interesting, you will attract the wrong students (or not enough of the right ones). Alumni will donate to more worthy causes. Faculty will go elsewhere. As will research grants. You may have one of the most distinctive educational experiences in the world, one that shapes kids into being highly creative, incredibly grounded pillars of their community. But if nobody knows about it, you fail. We don't mean to suggest that you'll be barring the doors anytime soon, but every time a kid who would be the perfect student for your school goes elsewhere because he or she didn't recognize what you had to offer—because he or she didn't understand your story—your brand has failed to do its job.

Now let's get back to those disgruntled tenured humanities professors from the beginning of the chapter. More often than not, their reluctance to trust a branding agency comes from the perception that branding is all about "selling" something, that an agency is going to come in, tell them who it is, and make up some pithy tagline that tries to sum it all up, but it will all be a lie—that it's "not true here." Maybe they had a bad past experience that ultimately failed. And that's the case when a brand is wrong. When the stories you tell as an organization are unclear, or worse, muddled in half-truths and closely guarded perceptions that are only held by a select few, the brand itself is untrue. In those cases, students who were misled into enrolling will soon realize they were sold a bill of goods, and will take their tuition dollars elsewhere, and will likely tell anyone who will listen that the school is "not what the brochures promised."

Or maybe they're frustrated because nobody ever came to them to ask their opinion on what distinguishes the school. More often than not, internal frustrations arise over the fact that people feel left out of the conversation. That's why you should always make a point of including as many faculty as possible in research sessions, or at least make sure there is departmental representation.

In the best cases, when the university community can come to an agreement on who they are and what they can stand for, and can confidently prove it with countless stories that back up that identity, students who identify with that philosophy will be naturally drawn to it like moths to a flame, or Apple fans to a Cupertino keynote. (OK, that's our last Apple reference in this book. Pinky swear.)

◇

Do the research. Find out what makes you and your values different than everyone else. Get everyone internally to understand this difference. Then invest in shouting it from the rooftops, over and over, in every way possible. Congratulations, you're branding.

Realize, however, no matter how good you are at reaching a consensus, you will always have some who want to tell their own stories. Some mean well, but don't understand the story, and need guidance. Others are openly defiant of any message the school communicates, and tell their own stories, which may only be true to their personal subjective situation—not the school as a whole. In the corporate world, good companies hire the right people and fire the wrong ones. Universities, however, have thrived for centuries by bringing differing viewpoints together to spark discussion. Everyone thinks their way is the best way, but if an individual is not being completely honest about the mission of the school in order to further his or her own goals, he or she is essentially lying to kids and stealing their tuition before the kids ultimately drop out. You can work hard to get everyone to understand why organizational cohesiveness benefits everyone, but there are still those who persist in pushing forward with their own agenda. In cases like this, don't try and muffle their opinions—just make sure your voice is louder than theirs. They'll hopefully turn their attentions (or get a job) elsewhere.

DON'T ADVERTISE

(YET.)

You wouldn't invite people over for a party in your home until you've had a chance to tidy up the place. Same goes for branding. Before you put the word out, make sure you've got the house in order. That means everyone internally understanding the message and agreeing to it. It means taking care of some of your most important communications materials first, like your website and your viewbook. It also means waiting as long as possible before running an ad campaign. We get it: your board of trustees likes to see TV commercials—it's proof that their budget is being spent on something. But schools rarely have the budgets to 1) properly make a good TV ad, one that can hold its own against the multi-million-dollar spots for Old Spice and Volvo running before and after it and 2) air it often enough so people will remember it. Ad campaigns also immediately bring out the critic in everyone. After all, we've all been exposed to thousands of hours of commercials all our lives, which makes everyone an immediate expert on how to make a good ad.

It's far better to start with something smaller that can get big results quickly. For most schools, we recommend rolling out a new brand in an undergraduate viewbook. It's substantial enough that it gives you more than 30 seconds to tell your story, and is seen by virtually every prospective student—and there is no better stat to point your board to than increased inquiries and applications. A great viewbook can give everyone in your organization something they can hold in their hands, read, and come away with an understanding of what your new brand represents.

You may hear some grumblings when you don't deliver a spot or campaign in the first quarter, but you'll have a piece that can be far more effective at delivering results, and can lay the foundation for everything else your brand is based on. Go with a 30-second spot with a pithy slogan, and you'll likely get taken as seriously as body spray (especially if you don't publicly reveal the spot until halftime of your homecoming football game, as one major school recently did, to a chorus of tens of thousands of boos after it aired on the stadium scoreboard).

Carnegie classifications and their ilk are meaningless to those outside of your organization. There are so many competing and conflicting ways to rank universities, and so much effort is wasted on trying to game the systems and artificially boost numbers instead of focusing on improving the institution from within. For better or for worse, however, people still rely on these rankings for everything from where to send their kids to where a top-ranked professor should go to do her research, so their importance can't be overlooked. What many schools forget, though, is that there's no magic bullet to propel you to the top. Instead of looking for ways to improve your rankings, look for ways to improve how people perceive you. If your brand is truthful, and you're persistent in getting the word out to audiences both internal and external, you'll find that the tide raises all ships, and a natural improvement in rankings is likely to follow.

It's also important to keep in mind that communicating to your peers is just as influential for improving your rankings as bringing in a strong class or shoring up your endowment through alumni donations. How good are you at making visiting faculty feel welcome on your campus? How often do you send your alumni magazine or president's report out to influencers in your field? What are your relations like with the media? Are they writing the right stories about you? Remember, every impression you make influences the perception people have of you.

HOW
DO YOU
GET TO

CARNEGIE

?

PRACTICE

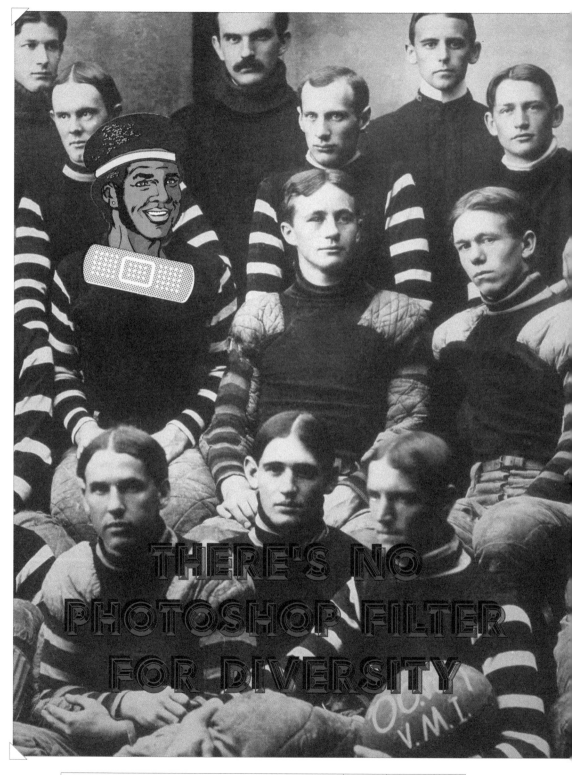

THERE'S NO PHOTOSHOP FILTER FOR DIVERSITY

Early in our discovery phase with a new school that hired us, we asked a classroom full of students if there was anything we felt could be better communicated to next year's freshmen.

"Don't lie to kids in your brochures," one minority student pleaded. "There aren't that many black kids here."

It's good advice. Schools walk a fine line on how to feature minority students in their marketing materials. Many overcompensate by including too many ethnic students. Maybe they think it's the quickest route to actually being more diverse. Maybe they just want something they can point to and say "see, here's a black woman, right on page two" when somebody questions them on it. In any case, schools should work hard to feature an appropriate, population-supported mix of students. And be wary of the three smiling students ("the white kid, the Asian girl, and the black guy") sitting under the majestic elm on the quad, laptops open. It's a cliché, and nobody's buying it.

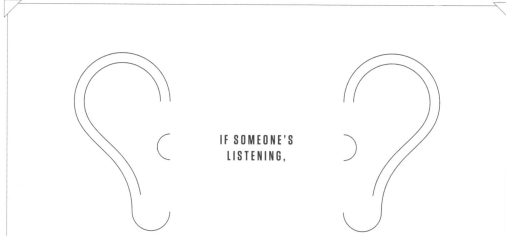

IF SOMEONE'S
LISTENING,

YOU HAVE A BRAND.

Your audience's perception is your brand. If someone is paying attention to you, be flattered, then take that opportunity to be as warm and truthful and engaging as possible.

There are other schools out there that are pretty much like yours, they're just not good at telling people about it. Instead of constantly trying to tell people you're 100 percent unique, celebrate the fundamental truth of what makes you distinctive, and own it.

THEY'RE NOT JUST BUYING AN EDUCATION,

THEY'RE BUYING A HOME.

AT LEAST FOR THE NEXT FOUR YEARS.

Make sure you're telling kids why they will want to live on your campus. Most schools have traditions that have bonded students together for decades, or at least a few years. Whatever they are, celebrate them. Even the weird ones. And if you don't have any, you better start some. You'll want to remind your future alumni of those warm memories when you're communicating your brand to them.

ARE YOU LOCATED

WITHIN A HALF HOUR

OF A BEACH?

Tell people.

Your best assets are often overlooked or taken for granted. Even if you felt like you've told the same story a thousand times, there's still someone who hasn't heard it yet.

If a school is really good at what they do, its alumni will feel fulfilled 10, 20, 30 years after graduation. Isn't that the ultimate measure of a school's success? We bet there's a small school out there that is better at preparing students for a lifetime of happiness than all the Harvards, Oxfords, and Stanfords combined. So how come nobody's measuring this?

PENCILS

You can look at all the research and findings in the world in an effort to "think" about branding—so much so that research paralysis begins to set in. As much as there's power in numbers, every research effort reaches a point of diminishing returns. The best know when to stop studying and take the next step forward and start making things, not more PowerPoints.

DOWN.

2

PROPER PLANNING

PREVENTS PISS POOR PERFORMANCE:

PROCESS

Choose
your own
adventure.

Convinced you can benefit from branding? Good, now all you need is a tagline and you're on your way.

Well, not really, but you'd be surprised how many schools think it's that easy. Schools have attempted to tackle brand development in countless different ways, but through experience (and a fair amount of misadventure) we've been able to hone college and brand development into a fairly concrete process—something 160over90 handily refers to as "The Process."

First, a disclaimer: You may have some great marketing resources in house to tackle branding on your own. Good for you—you're one of a select few. Even some of the world's most successful and recognizable brands (see Nike, Coke, et al.) with robust internal capabilities often rely on outside branding firms to help them augment their capabilities and to provide an outsider's perspective. Bringing in outside experts to assist in brand development is one of the surest ways to success, but it's certainly not the only way. In the interest of this not coming off as self-serving, we want to remind you that hiring us is not the only path to organization-wide enlightenment, but if you follow our recommendations, you'll hopefully find the partner that's right for you.

The recommended process breaks down into a convenient and well-rounded 10 steps:

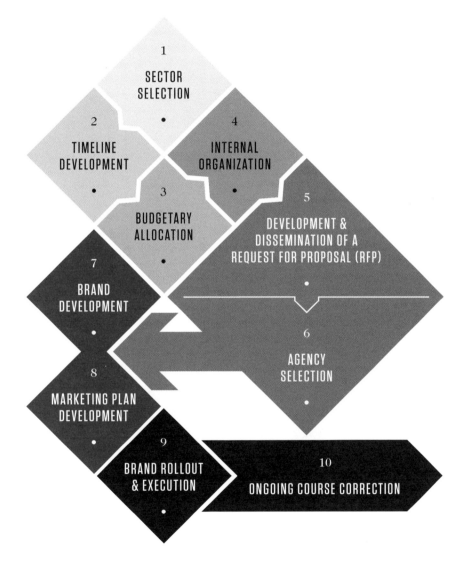

Now let's go into some detail about each of the above steps.

1

SECTOR
SELECTION

When we first started working with local Philadelphia colleges in the early-2000s, we were often asked to come in and work exclusively with undergraduate recruitment, and it's there that we found some early success. We'd developed a wealth of knowledge about the teen market working with lifestyle brands like American Eagle Outfitters and AND 1 (a basketball apparel brand), and we found a lot of parallels between selling a pair of jeans or sneakers to a 17-year-old, and helping them see themselves on a particular college campus (though the price points between the two were admittedly a bit different).

As we looked at the higher ed marketplace, we saw a lot of institutions saying the same things as their direct competitors, usually in bland, generic marketing materials that seemed to completely ignore their audience. We saw an opportunity to change the game and bring the conversation to kids on their terms, using bold graphic design and engaging copywriting that not only informed, but entertained. And we were successful. We were watching inquiries, applications, yield, SAT scores, and retention all rise at our partner institutions. But we were frustrated that we couldn't translate that success to other departments within our schools. While we were pouring the universities' hearts and souls into their undergrad marketing materials, we were watching their graduate, alumni relations, institutional advancement, and athletic departments flounder along with the same disjointed materials they had been using for decades. Whenever we inquired about translating our brand to these other departments we were often met with excuses. "Oh, they have their own thing, and their own budgets." "We've tried that before, and it didn't work." "You don't want to work with them. They're all nuts." It was clear to us that most schools were set up like garrulous medieval fiefdoms, with each department putting walls up around their individual efforts, and protecting their budgets like their wintertime grain stores.

A number of 160over90 success numbers.

ADMITTED STUDENTS

UNIVERSITY OF DAYTON

RANKED #1 IN HIGH SCHOOL CLASS

140% ↑

U.S. NEWS & WORLD REPORT RANKING

UNIVERSITY OF DAYTON
BROKE INTO THE
TOP 10
CATHOLIC UNIVERSITIES
FOR THE FIRST TIME EVER

UNDERGRADUATE INQUIRIES

LOYOLA UNIVERSITY MARYLAND

85% ↑

OUT-OF-STATE ENROLLMENT

331

CHESTNUT HILL COLLEGE
% ↑

FROM 8 STATES TO 20 STATES

COMMERCIALS ON YOUTUBE

MICHIGAN STATE UNIVERSITY

22,500 VIEWS

299 LIKES : 1 DISLIKE

ADVERTISING CAMPAIGN IMPRESSIONS

204
MILLION IMPRESSIONS

**PLUS, NATIONAL MEDIA COVERAGE
FROM ABC, FOX, MTV, USA TODAY,
THE NEW YORK TIMES, AND NPR.**

INTERNATIONAL STUDENT ENROLLMENT

WILKES UNIVERSITY

820%

INCREASE IN INTERNATIONAL DIVERSITY

37
FOREIGN COUNTRIES

UNDERGRADUATE APPLICATIONS

339% ↑
CHESTNUT HILL COLLEGE

40% ↑
LOYOLA UNIVERSITY MARYLAND

37% ↑
UNIVERSITY OF DAYTON

2008: LARGEST NUMBER OF APPS IN 160 YEAR HISTORY

9% ↑
IN ONE YEAR

MIAMI UNIVERSITY

UNDERGRADUATE ACCEPTANCE RATE

DOWN 19%
LOYOLA UNIVERSITY MARYLAND

AVERAGE S.A.T. SCORE

+40
POINTS

UNIVERSITY OF DAYTON

GRADUATE CREDITS

5,634 CREDITS

14% ↑
CHESTNUT HILL COLLEGE

PERCEPTION OF HIGHER ED. PEERS

81%

PEERS PARTICIPATING IN FOCUS GROUP AGREED THE NEW BRAND IMPROVED THEIR IMPRESSION OF

MICHIGAN STATE UNIVERSITY

WEB SITE ONLINE APPLICATIONS

LOYOLA.EDU

26%
INCREASE IN ONLINE APPS

45%
INCREASE IN UNIQUE VISITS

We tried for years to break down these walls, with limited success, until one day we decided to try an experiment. Well, to be fair, the experiment was kind of thrust in our lap. University of Dayton had hired us to rebrand their undergraduate recruitment materials, and when their applications jumped 37 percent in their first year of working with us, their president, Dr. Dan Curran, saw an opportunity to rebrand every sector of the university, including the graduate school, the UD School of Law, institutional advancement, athletics, and the University of Dayton Research Institute. Dr. Curran and his tremendous team challenged us to execute a complete rebrand of the institution from the top down, affecting each and every department within the institution.

Not going to lie: It was a difficult task to retrofit an existing undergraduate brand against the other sectors within the university. We had our share of doubters too, who thought the school's Marianist philosophy didn't really manifest itself within their program or department, or that their audience didn't really care about it. But we soon found that the school's educational approach provided a guiding hand throughout the university, even when those in charge weren't conscious of its presence. And as we began to translate that philosophy in meaningful and relevant ways to each audience, we saw a unified message begin to permeate the school, even affecting how Dr. Curran speak about the school in public.

Why do we think an institution-wide rebrand is the only one worth doing? Imagine the benefits of having all departments speaking with one voice, telling stories that speak to the organization's philosophy as a whole, while tailoring their brand to showcase each department's individual attributes. Your brand becomes so much more efficient, the fiefdoms break down just a little, and your dollars go further. All departments at the University of Dayton are now structured to share a common internal communications staff who knows how to tailor the university's message to various audiences to great effect, and they continue to rely on us to bring new innovation through additional initiatives.

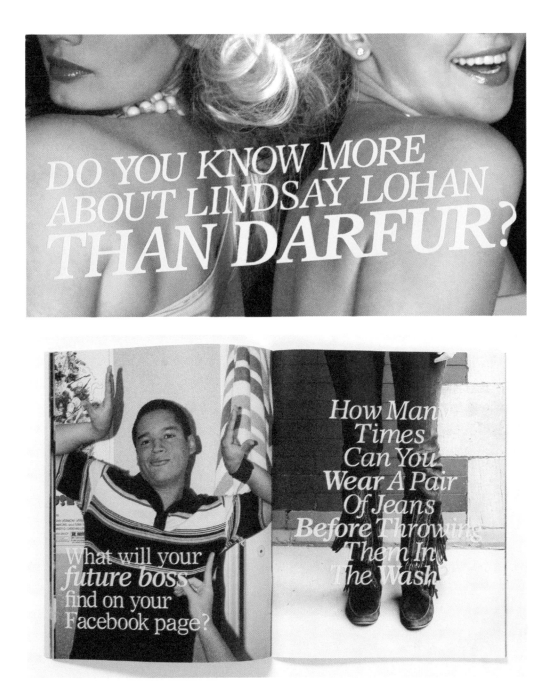

+ ABOVE Interior pages of the University of Dayton Viewbook.

DEFINE YOUR TERMS.

Beginning to think about your unique perspective is the first step to figuring out what school is best for you—and everyone agrees that coming to this conclusion is not a simple process.

YOU'VE GOT OPTIONS. EXAMINE THEM.

TEAM

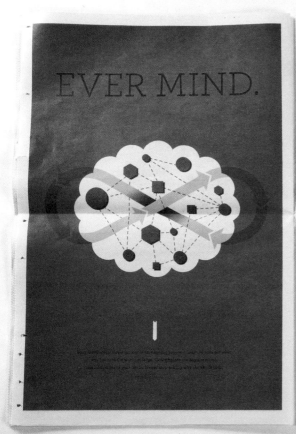

EVER MIND.

GET FIT.

Your physical well-being is the foundation for every experience you have. Tune your body, test your limits, and explore different ways to engage physically with the world. Exercise your power to improve yourself.

The process was put to the test when Loyola College in Maryland was undergoing a designation change to become Loyola University Maryland, and asked us to develop and implement a comprehensive rebrand of the school in a very short amount of time. Six months later, in their arena, the school flipped the switch on the new brand, figuratively, and quite literally, when they launched the new website live on the Jumbotron in front of several thousand people, including the Archbishop of Baltimore. Loyola's new brand affected everything from their recruitment materials to their signage, to their alumni magazine and their athletics media guides. Creating a brand under such a pressure test was an awesome and terrifying task, but the hugely positive outcome gave us such an amazing perspective on how best to roll out a university-wide brand.

You don't need to change your name to accomplish what Loyola achieved, but you do need a strong team and a lot of organization. If you choose to focus on your entire organization rather than a single department, your first step should be to identify the sectors that will participate in the rebrand, and get the key stakeholders from each sector involved. For most schools, there are the Big Four: undergraduate, graduate, alumni relations/institutional advancement, and athletics. We've also worked with marquee schools that have become their own juggernauts, like Loyola's Sellinger School or the University of Dayton School of Law. You may also have a department focused on corporate relations or a research institute. Perhaps student services needs its own message. Whatever the case, you should select your sectors based on those who have the greatest effect on achieving your institution's missions and goals. It doesn't hurt if they're also your biggest revenue generators.

Once these sectors have been selected and a key stakeholder for each has been identified, it's on to...

+ P. 50 Loyola University Maryland Search Piece, printed on newsprint.

2

TIMELINE
DEVELOPMENT

Set a date for when you'd like to have the new brand introduced. For most schools, this revolves around an admissions cycle or the fiscal year. Whatever your preference, we often advise schools to allow for double the amount of time they think it will take to organize themselves. It should take your agency no more than 12 weeks from the time you ink the contract until the time you begin to develop materials within the new brand, but the up-front work conducted before the agency is brought in usually takes much longer than most anticipate. That is, unless your organization is completely without bureaucracy, in which case you should put this book down now, as you're likely a temple of Buddhist monks in no need of a brand.

3

BUDGETARY

ALLOCATION

As an institute of higher education, your reputation is your greatest asset. Your brand shapes that reputation, and can have an immediate and direct effect on the students and faculty you recruit, how engaged you are with your alumni (and how much they donate), your institutional rankings, and your ability to thrive overall. The talents of your great faculty could be wasted if the world isn't made aware of their accomplishments.

That said, you should dedicate as much as possible to your branding and marketing efforts, as much as your organization can tolerate. There's no perfect number, but higher education has typically spent much less than its corporate counterparts. The industry is waking up, though, especially in the for-profit world of higher ed. According to PBS's "Frontline," the University of Phoenix spent $130 million on ads in 2008! Few, if any, traditional institutions could ever hope to approach that number, but the schools who continue to spend a few hundred thousand here and there each year are getting left in the dust, and quickly. Of course, spending more does not equate to success, but as more and more institutions become savvy to the ways of branding, the ones who choose not to compete in the marketplace could be the ones struggling the most as students and parents become smarter about where they send their tuition checks.

You also need to foster a culture where the funding of your branding efforts is not looked at as an operational cost, but as a capital expense. It has tangible value, should last for at least three-to-five years before requiring an overhaul, and could have more of a lasting effect on your institution than a new dorm or parking garage. The branding budget must be centralized, and success criteria need to be in place to constantly monitor progress.

Don't think your school can afford to brand properly? Maybe you should look at the situation from another angle. What internal resources do you have, and how much of a load can they lift? How much could individual departments and programs save by centralizing their efforts and pooling their budgets? By taking a 30,000-foot audit of what your school is spending on its communication efforts, you're likely to find that you're already spending much more than you thought, but those resources are spread thin among a wide variety of initiatives, many of which are inefficient and ineffective, not to mention outside of your core brand message. Focus those internal efforts, corral the dollars together, and you might be surprised at what you can accomplish with what was formerly a meager marketing budget. Your reputation is more important than your athletic facilities or that new LEED-certified science building or dorm you just put up.

WITHOUT YOUR REPUTATION, THOSE BUILDINGS WOULD BE EMPTY SHELLS.

4

INTERNAL
ORGANIZATION

Let's lay it out there: Some schools aren't ready for branding. Surprise!

If any of the situations below sound familiar, stop. Maybe your money would be better focused elsewhere. We'll try not to make this sound like a mid-90s Jeff Foxworthy monologue.

---- ⊘ ----

IF YOUR PRESIDENT DOESN'T BELIEVE IN BRANDING

IF YOUR STRATEGIC PLAN AND MASTER PLAN HAVE BEEN
"WORKS IN PROGRESS" FOR THREE YEARS OR MORE

IF YOUR VP-LEVEL STAFF IS IN AGREEMENT
NOT TO SELF-SABOTAGE THE PROCESS

IF YOU'RE NOT PREPARED TO PROPERLY FUND THE EFFORTS,
OR IF INDIVIDUAL DEPARTMENTS AND SECTORS ARE
UNWILLING TO POOL AND SHARE RESOURCES

IF NOBODY IN YOUR ORGANIZATION WANTS TO TAKE
OWNERSHIP OR RESPONSIBILITY FOR THE BRAND, OR IF
YOU HAVE NOBODY IN PLACE TO PROPERLY MANAGE IT

IF MOST PEOPLE THINK
"OUR CURRENT STUFF IS GOOD ENOUGH"

IF YOU'RE NOT PREPARED FOR THE FACT THAT
WHATEVER YOU DO WILL BE UNACCEPTABLE TO ONE OUT
OF EVERY FIVE PEOPLE IN YOUR ORGANIZATION

IF YOU'RE LOOKING AT BRANDING LIKE
IT'S A SHORT SPRINT INSTEAD OF THE NEVER-ENDING
TRIATHLON IT REALLY IS

---- ⊘ ----

Branding is not right for everyone. It takes a strong stomach for criticism, a long-term commitment in dollars, and support from the top down. If you don't have a president willing to stand up in front of his harshest critics and be able to say "this is who we are, I support it, and I hope you will too," any new brand message you develop will have the impact of a firecracker tossed into the Pacific. Likewise if your board or executive council is in constant disagreement with your institution's goals. (We've seen it. Our relationship ended badly.) Or if you believe that a brand can move your school forward, but nobody's willing to stand by your side. You're doomed for failure—and you should probably seek employment from people who care.

If that's not an option, you need to start playing politics. Start pushing your agenda on the president. Once that's sold in, rely on her to be a powerful ally as you work on the VPs and the board. Demand a solid commitment not just in words, but in dollars.

If nothing seems to be working, the last thing you should do is put your head down and plow away. You'll waste a lot of money on a shoddy, noisy (or quiet) brand.

Now that those unpleasantries are out of the way, let's say you're not among the directionless throngs above and are ready to push off from the shore.

You must have someone in your organization willing to be the brand champion. If you're reading this book, maybe that's you. Your branding effort needs to be centralized with a single person willing to roll with the punches—which at times will come fast and furious. For many institutions, centralizing branding and marketing is a foreign concept, which strikes us as strange, since universities centralize everything from food services to who orders tees for the golf team.

The first thing to put in place is a stakeholder committee. Assemble a group of those who believe in branding and are willing to stick it out. Every organization is different, but a few key people to include can be:

A VP OF COMMUNICATIONS OR MARKETING

THE VP OF UNDERGRADUATE ENROLLMENT

THE VP OF GRADUATE ENROLLMENT

VP OF PUBLIC/MEDIA RELATIONS

ATHLETIC DIRECTOR

VP OF ALUMNI RELATIONS/INSTITUTIONAL ADVANCEMENT

DEANS OF MAJOR SCHOOLS

VP OF RESEARCH (IF APPLICABLE)

AND OF COURSE, THE PRESIDENT AND PROVOST

This list is not all-encompassing, but it's important to include those who shape the overall vision for the school, and those who share the responsibility for disseminating the message to their wide-ranging internal audiences.

It's also important to consider the size and scope of your rebrand. If you only plan on focusing your communications to an undergraduate audience, build your committee accordingly.

If you're planning on rolling out a message institution-wide, then make sure every sector within your institution is represented from the beginning. The last thing a director wants is to have a brand message thrust upon them after it's already been through several iterations, approvals, and buy-ins.

Finally, do you have the time to make sure that whoever's responsible for the marketing in each sector is adhering to the brand, is meeting internal and external deadlines, and is rolling out materials as planned? Didn't think so. Consider hiring a Marketing Manager to be the daily liaison between each sector and your branding firm. The Marketing Manager can help in routing each round of work to the right people, making sure everyone adheres to schedules, and can help the agency get answers to any questions that might come up.

BRAND MANAGEMENT MODEL

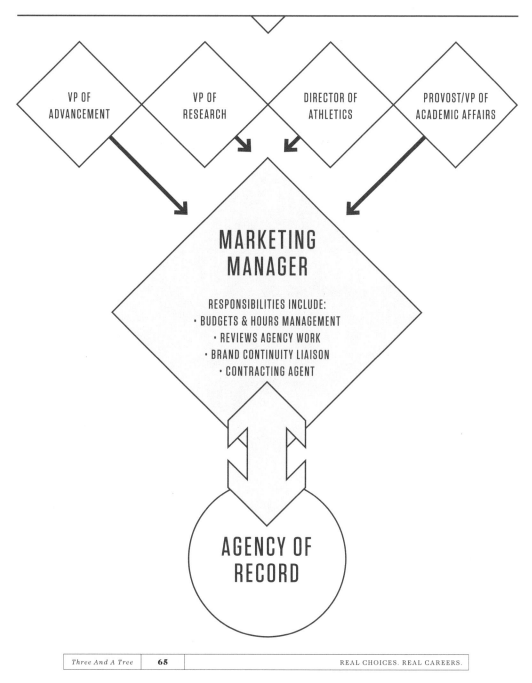

VP OF
ADVANCEMENT

VP OF
RESEARCH

DIRECTOR OF
ATHLETICS

PROVOST/VP OF
ACADEMIC AFFAIRS

MARKETING MANAGER

RESPONSIBILITIES INCLUDE:
- BUDGETS & HOURS MANAGEMENT
- REVIEWS AGENCY WORK
- BRAND CONTINUITY LIAISON
- CONTRACTING AGENT

AGENCY OF RECORD

5

DEVELOPMENT & DISSEMINATION OF AN RFP

With an internal team in place, your next step is to conduct a search for a research and branding firm that can help you determine and focus your message for your various sectors. Occasionally, there may be people on your team who have worked and had success with particular firms in the past. Be sure and ask around to see if anyone has strong recommendations. You may be able to easily find firms who you may determine to be a good fit, often with little more than an introductory meeting. Otherwise, your next best option is to issue a Request For Proposals (RFP).

An RFP is a brief distributed to potential partners detailing what you hope to accomplish, your needs from a firm, the scope of your assignment (length of partnership and size of the job), and the budget you have to work with. You should consider what deliverables you hope to ultimately obtain from your firms, but be sure and give your partners leeway to come in and make recommendations on what they believe the best solutions could be. The best branding agencies are problem solvers first, and order takers second, and if you dictate too strongly what you hope to see from them, you may be leaving better solutions off the table.

We won't go into great detail about how to formally conduct an RFP process, as most institutions are well versed in this from past experience. But we will say that most RFPs agencies receive are sparse on detail, and rarely include important information like budgetary limitations. There are plenty of examples of good RFPs online, and some universities regularly post their RFPs online, so there's a wealth of good information there. On several occasions, we've even helped universities write their RFPs, so if you really get in a bind, don't hesitate to call one of the agencies you're considering and ask them what they'd like to see in an RFP. By including the right information about your assignment, you're likely to get better responses. With responses in, make sure you take the time to meet with each of your top selections to go over their capabilities, review how they plan on structuring their job and their process, and finally, figure out if you, well, like them. After all, you're going to be spending some time together.

You'll notice that we suggested hiring both a research firm and a branding firm. Why? There are a number of terrific research firms out there who do a great job of gathering quantitative data via interviews and competitive research, then parsing that information into a number of possible strategic directions that both accurately reflect who you are as an organization and differentiate you in the marketplace. They can also help you avoid possible pitfalls in how you talk to your audience.

Case in point: Prior to engaging us, one client worked with a research firm to determine that the school's mentoring culture was not only baked in to the school's educational philosophy, it also resonated with potential undergrads—more so than any other message the school tested. In reviewing the data, we could clearly see support for this message, but with one vital caveat: if you told kids they would be "mentored by their professors," they were clearly creeped out. How did we know? In a test of 10 messages, this one ranked dead last. But later in the study, we saw the same positioning was rephrased as "personal attention." In this case, kids marked this one as their favorite. This fascinating differentiation allowed us to go in and find a wealth of anecdotal information about how students were given a unique level of personal guidance from their professors and classmates, which we highlighted throughout marketing materials without once mentioning "mentoring." (OK, since the president of the school asked for it, we included it once.) But we gave it the proper context so it wouldn't be misunderstood. On the other hand, we found that the "mentoring" message tested very strongly with parents, so this term was used often in our communications directly to them.

Without this data in hand, we may have stumbled in the wrong direction and fallen flat on our faces instead of seeing the 11 percent increase in applications the school experienced after rolling out their new brand.

276 SEPARATE PARTS WORKING HARMONIOUSLY
TO CREATE YOUR TWO OUNCES OF ESPRESSO.

DeLonghi

delonghiusa.com

For an example from the consumer marketplace, take De'Longhi, a
100-year-old-plus family-owned Italian manufacturer of small appliances:
everything from high-end espresso machines to space heaters. Quantitative
research showed that their Italian design could be a huge asset, but the
client was reluctant to embrace it. To De'Longhi, Italian in America meant
Ragu, Olive Garden, The Sopranos. They didn't want to go anywhere
near those associations. Our qualitative discussions, though, found that
consumers were savvy enough to align the brand with other high-end
Italian brands like Ferrari, Prada, and Pellegrino—insight that led us to
hire a renowned photographer of Porsches to shoot our De'Longhi blenders.

+ ABOVE De'Longhi advertising campaign.

6

AGENCY
SELECTION

Of course we have a vested interest in this, but we recommend bringing in a partner that not only has broad experience branding not just higher education or cultural institutions but in working with a wide variety of consumer clients as well. The most talented writers, designers, creative directors, public relations experts, and interactive designers and programmers typically prefer to work in creative environments where they're challenged and exposed to a wide variety of industries, rather than getting pigeonholed into one particular niche. The same teams who work on our university accounts are also developing solutions for clients like Nike and Mercedes-Benz, so they're constantly approaching their work with fresh perspectives, and it seems like our clients appreciate the ideas they bring to the table. Offering our employees this diversity allows us to hire the best staff possible, and helps us avoid the creative burnout that can come from cranking out search piece after search piece.

But we're not the only one. There are plenty of firms like us out there with a great mix of expertise, so conduct your search carefully. Make sure you find a partner who is committed to sticking with you through thick and thin. There are some agencies who'd rather avoid the delicate and often intense political negotiations that come with brand development at the college and university level, and prefer clients who are "easier" to work with. (A sure sign of this is an agency who wants to jump right to an ad campaign.) Have your agency by your side to help sell the work through to all your levels of constituents, even when the going gets tough, instead of dropping off some work and wishing you all the best. We've worked with plenty of schools that hired "hit-and-run" shops that weren't willing to deal with the bureaucracy of higher ed, who later called us to help them pick up the pieces. Never pleasant.

Once you have narrowed down your list of potential agencies to a select few, bring them in to interview with your selection committee. Ask them to present case studies of relevant work, and try and determine if these are people you'd like to work with for the next several years. But here's a big pitfall to avoid: Don't ask them to pitch work. We know it's tempting, but it's damn near impossible to come up with the right strategy or creative solution based on the limited information in an RFP or a follow-up phone call. The work you receive from all respondents will likely be far off the mark, and will lack the insight that only comes from the upfront research conducted by the agency you ultimately hire. You wouldn't ask a lawyer or accountant to do free work for you without getting to know you, so why would you ask a branding firm?

If you feel you absolutely must see work tailored to your organization before you can make a decision, be prepared to pay for it, and allow your shortlisted agencies time and access to your staff in order to fully understand your institution and the challenges you face. What we find almost all the time, however, is that schools who go this route often choose the same firm they would have selected based on an interview and thorough portfolio review alone, but they ended up tripling the time and cost it would have normally taken to make the selection, and spent a valuable portion of their budget on work from other firms that is ultimately thrown away.

HERE'S A BIG PITFALL TO AVOID:

DON'T ASK THEM TO PITCH WORK

7

BRAND
DEVELOPMENT

This is something you'll rarely hear from someone in our industry: It's not always about the work. Now that you've made the tough decision on selecting a research agency, a branding agency, or both, you now need to undergo a period of learning and discovery to find out what are not only the fundamental truths about your organization, but also how to make those truths distinctive and relevant to all of your various audiences. The quantitative data and analysis conducted by a research firm can be a great first step, but be prepared for this process to take six months or more. The firm will want to conduct hundreds of interviews at all levels of your organization in order to make their recommendations, so open your doors. Once the firm has analyzed its numbers and presented its work, you'll want to share it—not only to get early buy-in from your various constituents, but also to let your president and your board know how their money's being spent. When people make the decision to participate in a rebrand, and they don't see billboards up by the end of the first month, they start coming out of the woodwork to gently inquire as to what's taking you so long. Make sure they know that you're trying to determine just what it is that makes your institution stand out before investing in the wrong message, and they'll hopefully cool their jets.

After the quantitative research is conducted, it's time to involve your branding firm, and don't hold anything back. Share all the data and results (both good and bad) you can with them, and they'll be able to head off with some good initial direction.

The work we develop for higher ed institutions is always tailored individually toward the challenges they face, but our process is always the same.

First we take what we've learned to date, and develop a detailed questionnaire for each sector, and conduct several days of interviews with people at all levels of the organization. At this point, at least one department usually asks why we're asking more questions. After all, isn't this what they already went through with the research firm? Our research, however, is strictly qualitative, and conducted for very different reasons: We're trying to validate what we've learned from you to date, and determine through interviews and observation what distinguishes you. More so, can we prove it? Is it true? How can we relate these truths in the most interesting way possible?

With so many institutions of higher ed out there, the surface-level factors typically used to differentiate colleges are not so distinctive as everyone thinks. Many schools primarily identify themselves as Catholic (as if that says it all), but there are nearly 1,900 Catholic universities and institutions around the world. Of course, Catholicism isn't a one-size-fits-all proposition, so many schools identify themselves by a particular religious order, such as Jesuit (of which there are 28 institutions in the U.S.) or Franciscan (20) or Marianist (3). Now, we haven't run into many 17-year-olds who can explain the finer points of philosophical or religious differentiation between these orders, and the schools themselves typically do a rather poor job of explaining them. This point came to light when we began working with the University of Dayton. Despite its public-sounding name, UD is a Catholic school, and is one of the three Marianist schools in the U.S. When we initially interviewed Dayton about why a kid should choose them over, say, their Ohio competitor Xavier, we were told "our Marianist educational philosophy." Problem was, each person we interviewed had a different perspective on what that philosophy was all about. Even the Marianist Brothers at Dayton themselves struggled with pinning down a consistent, mutually agreed-upon answer. It wasn't until we had a face-to-face interview with a Marianist professor, however, that we discovered something interesting. Unlike many professors, Marianists, we were told, are the first to admit that they don't have all the answers. This humility allows them to approach the world with an open mind and tackle problems not as individuals, but in a community. Combine this with a particular Midwestern sensibility, and you get an atmosphere at the University of Dayton where you can approach the world with eyes open and a willingness to ask some tough questions that you may never learn the answer to. We knew we were on to something, so we tested this message in interviews with everyone from current students to the president, Dr. Dan Curran. Before long, we knew we had our brand, and that message has now been rolled out in every sector of UD. But it wouldn't have been possible if we weren't able to ask some pretty tough questions up-front in the initial phase of discovery.

After allowing several weeks for discovery research and interviews, your next step for your agency should be the development of a creative brief. The creative brief is a two-page distillation of everything learned during the discovery, and is the blueprint that agencies use to make sure their message remains on-the-mark throughout the brand development process. The keystone of a creative brief is what many firms call a key message or a Unique Selling Proposition (USP). This is a one-sentence summary of just what it is that makes your institution special—essentially what you would want to tell someone about your school if you only had 15 seconds with them on an elevator—and should ultimately be the message you build upon for every touchpoint your university has with its audiences. Your USP should be simple and succinct. After all, who wants to try and communicate a message that has 15 different modifiers and clauses? Avoid the temptation to get the kitchen sink in there.

Oh, so you'd like an example? Let's start with a mission statement that wasn't specifically written for a university, creative brief, or even for an agency, but it's hard to beat its resonance:

> *"I believe that this nation should commit itself to achieving the goal, before this decade is out, of landing a man on the Moon and returning him safely to the Earth."*
>
> — President John F. Kennedy, May 1961

Now let's say we take that and craft it into a single-minded proposition that can be both our mission and our USP:

"We're going to the moon and back."

program) after JFK uttered his famous words, but it would be tough for anyone to not know what they were working toward. Which brings us to our next phase in brand development.

Working within the creative brief and USP, the agency should next tailor the USP to make it relevant for each of your sectors and their respective audiences, a "USP Cloud," where the basic structure of the overall USP is reworded to reflect what makes it meaningful for undergraduate, graduate, et al. If you were working with Kennedy's original USP for NASA, you might imagine our USP Cloud to look something like this:

NASA'S USP

▼

"WE'RE GOING TO THE MOON AND BACK."

ASTRONAUTS

▼

"We are training to fly a bucket of bolts to the moon, conduct some experiments, perhaps hit a golf ball or two, and hopefully make it back to Earth in one piece."

SCIENTISTS

▼

"We will test the effects of space travel on man, conduct experiments on the atmospheric and surface conditions on our Earth's moon, and analyze post-flight samples of moon rock."

AERONAUTICAL ENGINEERS

▼

"We develop rockets that will propel astronauts to the moon, landers that will transport them to the lunar surface, and orbiters and capsules that will bring them safely back to Earth."

VARIOUS TEST MONKEYS

▼

"We're space monkeys. We do what we're told."

Once the creative brief and USP Cloud are approved, our agency begins what is typically a six-week development of the conceptual executions (a.k.a., the work). First, we spend a week locked in a room, brainstorming various ways to convey the messages in the USP Cloud. We then narrow these down to two distinct big ideas, write a rationale for why we believe each one is correct, and begin to source visual inspiration for each. Once we have each direction solidified (in theory, at least), we develop what we refer to as Brand Art. Brand art is simply several theoretical layouts that include examples of how copy, photography, illustration, and graphic design can all come together to convey the idea. Once we're comfortable with the direction each idea is headed in, we then prove the idea against each sector within the institution against a wide variety of mediums, in what we call our Brand Concept. Again, these executions are purely hypothetical—none of it is real work. But it's constructed to ensure that the idea has legs; that it can work equally well in a viewbook spread for undergrads as it can in an alumni annual fund mailing. After this work is presented (typically 10-15 theoretical executions against each idea), excitement hopefully ensues. For the first time, our clients are able to see examples of what the brand looks, feels, and sounds like through design, copywriting, photography, illustration, and layout. We then work with them to determine which of the two concepts most clearly and creatively delivers the distinctiveness of the institution.

Hey, here's a 160over90 fun fact: The majority of the above paragraph is, in a nutshell, our secret steps numbers 2 and 3 in our Process that we sell to every school we work with. Why give it away? Well, there are some steps in there you may find useful. But be careful, in the wrong hands, a chainsaw becomes more than just a garden implement.

For an example of what one of our brand concepts looks like and how it takes shape, check out this post on our blog, The Boomerang Table, to get an idea:

WWW. 160VER90.COM/ BLOG/ LOYOLABRAND .HTML

The conceptual work typically goes through several rounds of refinement, before we move on to...

8

MARKETING PLAN

DEVELOPMENT

With an approved concept in place, now is the appropriate time for you and your agency to focus on the development of a marketing plan to determine how the new brand will be rolled out both internally and externally.

For most traditional marketers, a marketing plan is a pretty straightforward affair, usually wrapped around individual advertising campaigns or financial quarters: Here's what I want to make, and here's where I want to run it. For colleges and universities, the same basic rules apply, but things can get complicated quickly. How do you communicate with each audience? When will they be most receptive to my message? What do I want them to do after seeing my materials?

Take a typical alumni relations communications flow for example. A frequent lament of these departments is "we kind of need to reconnect with our audience." But which audience? Young alumni? Infrequent donors? Lapsed donors? The Big Money Folks? The major donors demand personal appeals from the president, while the young alums might prefer a phone call every once in a while (but not too often). And when is the right time to ask? Should you ask for donations in every edition of the alumni mag, before the reunion (or after), or should you send a letter only after a prolonged quiet phase of a capital campaign? The "reconnecting" problem often doesn't lie with infrequent contact, but is often a result of too much contact from someone with not a lot of new news, like an old high school friend constantly contacting you on Facebook to ask you "how's it going?" It's often the case too that one department might not know what another is up to, like the time one of our account managers got calls from her alma mater's 10-year reunion committee, a representative of the Annual Fund, and an assistant coach of the women's soccer team, all soliciting donations within a single week.

The development of each sector's marketing plan should be an annual ritual, and should be looked at as an opportunity for some spring cleaning. You and your agency should take a good, hard look at what materials you're currently sending out, but also look for opportunities you could be missing. Would it be more effective to distribute some materials online instead of through a costly print mailing? Would it be better to conduct a transfer campaign over the Thanksgiving holiday, when most new (and frustrated) college freshmen are home for break? Is there a big gap in your communications with high school students when they don't hear anything from you for more than a month? Work within each department (and your budget) to develop a plan that eliminates pieces that don't have an impact on your goals, and constantly strive to innovate with new pieces. And don't be afraid to challenge your agency to push their thinking too.

With each department's plan in place, your work isn't quite done. Cross-check your plans against one another. Can you save money by buying all the paper for athletics recruitment brochures and the graduate direct mail campaign at the same time? Can templates be created to hold a wider variety of more base-level communications? Is the graduate department doing anything to market its programs to senior undergraduates? By looking at the big picture all at once, you may come up with ways to become more efficient or effective in your communications.

MARKETING PLAN DEVELOPMENT IS AN AN ANNUAL RITUAL.

9

BRAND ROLLOUT
& EXECUTION

For each sector, we recommend beginning with a seminal piece that contains enough copy and graphic design to give everyone within that particular department a clear sense of the brand message and what it looks like via graphic design. It also helps if it's a piece with wide distribution so you can begin to get a sense of how it's received out in the real world (even better if it's a piece where you can measure response). Great examples of these seminal pieces are the viewbook for undergraduates, departmental brochures for graduates, alumni magazines for advancement, and recruitment kits or media plans for athletics. Once complete, these pieces can be the benchmark against which other pieces can be developed whether they're being executed by your agency or internal staff.

+ P.90-91 A selection of 160over90 higher education publication designs.

10

ONGOING COURSE

DIRECTION

No brand is perfect out of the gate. Goals change, new faculty arrives, and new programs are developed. Monitor your university's news feeds for fresh material for next year's viewbook, and don't be afraid to shift your marketing plan around to take advantage of new opportunities. If you have a solid message at your core, how you deliver that message always has room to improve. The day your new brand is implemented is the perfect time to start planning for when your brand changes. Did you think working in higher ed was going to be a cushy ride?

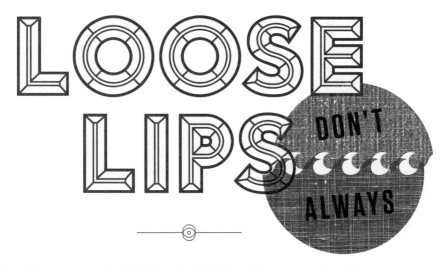

LOOSE LIPS DON'T ALWAYS

When a large corporation like Pepsi or UPS introduces a new brand, movement is swift. Company-wide conferences are held, internal memos are distributed, a road show is taken to district offices, and corporate campuses are plastered with banners and posters introducing the newly minted messaging for all to see. Packaging, delivery trucks, the main website, and advertising all change at the flip of a switch—seemingly overnight.

Colleges and universities—and the partners they select—often do a poor and irresponsible job of rolling out and communicating a new brand to internal audiences. People hear talk of a new brand in development, and after a few months, a few pieces here and there trickle out, maybe in a postcard or a billboard or some new business cards. After another few months, a viewbook hits the market. People who need to communicate the new brand (i.e., everyone within the organization) begin to get some clues as to what the new brand stands for, and their early efforts are muddled best-guess efforts. Perhaps some brand guidelines are developed, but only shared with a core group of communications staff. Athletics and graduate recruitment may have been left completely out of the loop, so when the new website is launched without their knowledge six months

later, their first reaction is typically befuddled frustration, which soon turns to criticism, so they continue to stubbornly soldier on with what's always seemed to work for them, which is wildly out-of-sync with the rest of the school's branding efforts. Then a big TV spot debuts, and the public reaction becomes a giant collective "What the hell was that?" No wonder some schools seem to change their brand with the weather.

Once your brand has been developed and approved by your internal stakeholder committee, your need to give your message escape velocity. EVERYONE within your organization should be able to summarize your brand positioning in a few sentences to anyone who asks. To get to this exalted plateau, we recommend holding brand camps and town hall meetings to introduce your efforts to your entire community.

THIS ONE TIME, AT

BRAND CAMP

ALL YOU CAN EA

Every school has an internal communications, marketing, and public relations staff who are on the front lines of disseminating messaging and materials created within the new brand. At a smaller school with a couple of thousand students, these responsibilities rest with as few as three people. At the larger schools, there may be 250 people or more. Regardless of size, a Brand Camp is a one-day summit where your agency can present the new brand messaging, show some examples of how the new brand can be used (usually about 15-20, covering every sector of the institution), offer demonstrations on how to execute some of the more complicated graphic design moves or write copy in the new tone, and allow at least an hour for Q&A. During this session, offer a link to an online version of the school's new brand guidelines, hosted prominently on the school's website. If you're a larger institution, consider break-out sessions for staff to meet with individual teams to give them some insight into how the overarching message for the school can be tailored to fit their needs. By the end of this meeting, the communications staff should understand why and how the new brand was developed so they can then move forward with continuing the message within their individual departments.

In every organization, you need to have both brand camps and town hall meetings. If you gathered a large group together and asked them what flavor of ice cream they'd like, you'll wind up with vanilla. Likewise with a brand. That's why it's so important to divide groups into both parties.

Decision makers are the ones, who, well, make decisions. They're in charge of gathering feedback from the influencers, parsing it, then turning it into useable feedback that everyone can use. They may choose to ignore some comments as unimportant details that could distract the team from the goal at hand, or they may make the decision to carry forth an idea to the rest of the team. What's important is that they listen and ultimately decide what can help a direction get better, and what's better left unsaid. The decision makers usually make up the core group at the top end of your steering committee.

Influencers are anyone in your organization with an opinion that needs to be heard and considered. They may be professors of important pro-grams, in-house designers, or a long-standing member of faculty. They should be included in key meetings from the beginning, and their thoughts should be carefully weighed. Conflicting opinions should be moderated by the decision makers, and passed on to those who are developing the brand. Dissension and dialogue are OK, just as long as someone takes on the role of being the final arbiter.

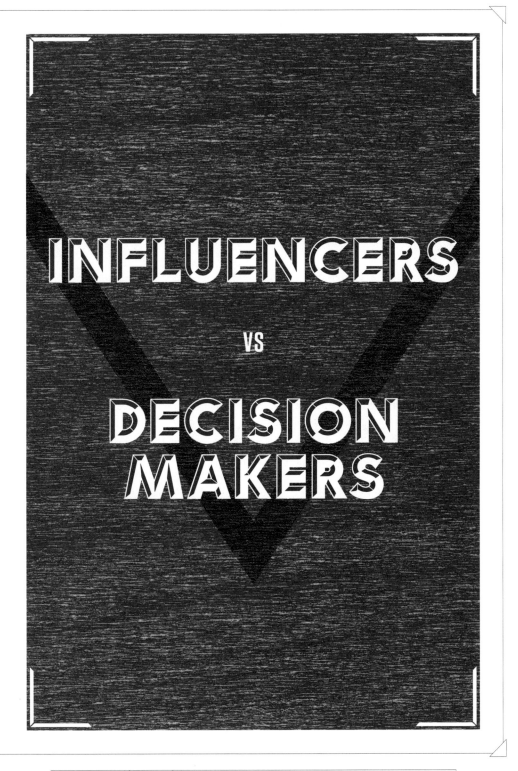

ANYONE WHO ANSWERS THE PHONE

To introduce the brand to the wider community, you may want to consider a succession of town hall meetings. Unlike brand camps, these meetings are less hands-on demonstration and more revelatory into the back story of how the brand was created, how it is being implemented, and what attendees can do to help get the message out. In one meeting, you may speak to all of the faculty of an individual business school, another might be attended by the entire admissions staff. At one school, we even met with every hourly employee of the institution, everyone from the cafeteria staff to the head landscaper. At the beginning of this meeting, you might ask the president to stand up in front of each group and talk about the new direction the university is moving in, why you're making the effort, and how the branding campaign is being carried out. In some cases, this may have been the only time the president has gotten up to talk to them personally, so this endorsement sets the stage for the brand to be introduced and taken to heart. Also during this meeting, you'll present the group with the new brand and all its forms, and remind everyone of the importance of "living the brand"—by internalizing it and making sure you find ways to bring it to your work and communicate it to the outside world. It could be

IS A BRAND STEWARD.

in the way you answer the phone, how you wear your work uniform, or some talking points you can use to describe the institution when recruiting faculty. Hopefully, staff leave town hall meetings energized and enthusiastic about the new brand, making your job that much easier. Sometimes, faculty is hesitant to embrace a new brand, and some might be outright pissed off—sometimes for good reason. Listen to their concerns, reiterate the importance of a brand, and ask them to be patient with you as you work out the kinks. Most often, they're just looking to voice their concerns or get some issues off their chest. With time, you'll hopefully have some promising results you can share, which can go a long way toward earning their trust.

Finally, the importance of getting students involved in the process from the beginning cannot be understated. Invite them to discovery meetings, share creative concepts with them, show them the work, and explain what the brand means to them. Offer town hall meetings to them at a time when as many students as possible can attend—not in the middle of a class-filled afternoon. If students understand and embrace the message, you'll have your most powerful, opinionated audience on your side.

you'll be able to share where you are in the brand development process,
showcase some of the early efforts, and highlight departments that are
successfully implementing the brand once it's developed.

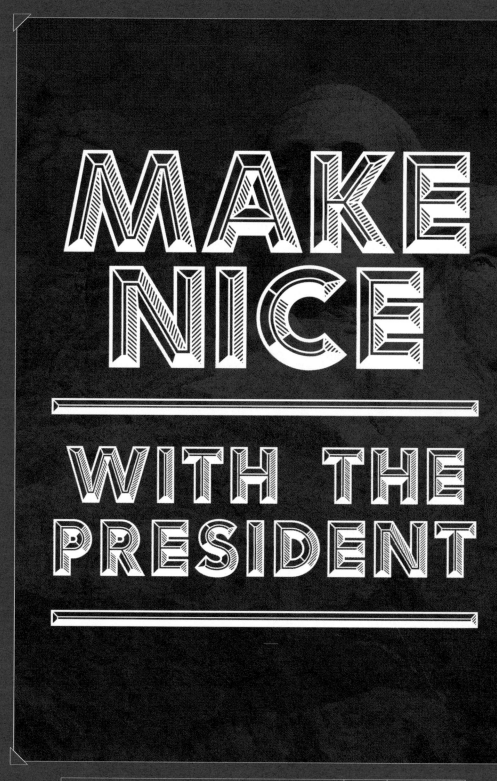

If you're in-charge of your marketing or branding you should directly report to the president. In fact, we often insist on it before engaging with a client. But what if you're not?

Get in with the Director of PR. Your reputation is your brand, and when the shit hits the fan, your president will turn to them. This is when your president needs you most. Use this opportunity.

BUY A BLIMP, ALREADY.

Give your agency room to innovate, and it might come up with some surprising ways to improve your brand. Here are a few non-traditional ideas that have been included in our marketing plans (not all of them were implemented):

PUBLIC SCULPTURE

SENDING ACCEPTED STUDENTS A BOX OF LAUNDRY SOAP

A PDF GENERATOR ALLOWING GRADUATE INDIVIDUAL PROGRAMS TO DEVELOP THEIR OWN BRANDED MATERIALS

INTERIOR DESIGN FOR AN ATHLETICS CLOSING ROOM

BLIMP (JUST $300,000 A MONTH!)

AIRPLANE BANNERS

MASCOT AMBUSHES

SEASON TICKET WELCOME KITS

A 360-DEGREE VIDEO VIRTUAL TOUR

BOBBLEHEADS

FAKE "NOT FOR SALE" YARD SIGNS FOR HOME MORTGAGES SAVED BY A UNIVERSITY EXTENSION PROJECT

SMART CAR FLEET

A BRANDED VENDING MACHINE SELLING INTERNATIONAL POWER CONVERTERS IN AIRPORTS (TO CONVEY THE SCHOOL'S "CONNECTIVITY")

A MULTIMEDIA HORSE TRAILER

UNTIL IT

◇◇◇◇◇

Students, faculty, and alumni will all hate your brand until they either get involved in the process or see evidence that it actually works. Don't build your marketing committee around yes-men. Include your harshest critics in the process from the beginning to keep them informed, and share your results frequently with everyone.

◇◇◇◇◇

WORKS.

YOUR LOGO SUCKS

DON'T CHANGE A THING.

The only university logos people can envision off the top of their head are for the athletic programs of schools like Notre Dame and the University of Texas. And that's just because they're on TV every Saturday during the school year and tattooed on fans across the country. Your logo is important, but don't change it just because you can. Focus on getting everything else in line first.

Every few years, test the effectiveness of your branding. Is it still relevant? Is it still true? Should it be altered to reflect changes to your institution? Is it beginning to feel dated compared to other brands (non-university) your audiences are being exposed to? Maybe it's time to get under the hood and make some modifications. Or if the research shows that it's not resonating, put in a new engine.

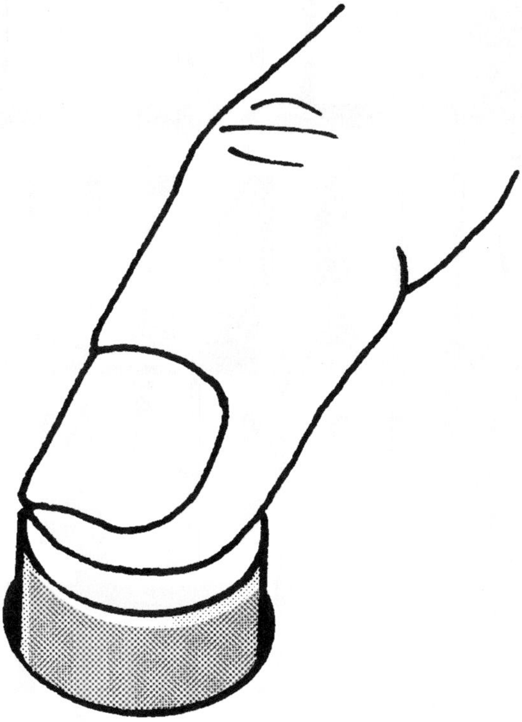

Ø

DON'T HIDE THE MONEY

○

Tell your agency exactly how much you have to spend on the creation of the brand, production, and media—then hold them to it. Hiding the true budget will result in presentations filled with ideas and concepts you can't really afford, or worse: breakthrough ideas held back for fear of overstepping an imaginary budget constraint.

DON'T HIRE AGENCIES LIKE YOU BUY TRASH CANS

A lot of public institutions send out RFPs for agencies, then hire the cheapest one after opening the proposals at a public meeting. A great way to buy toilet paper. Not so effective when you're trying to bring in outside expertise.

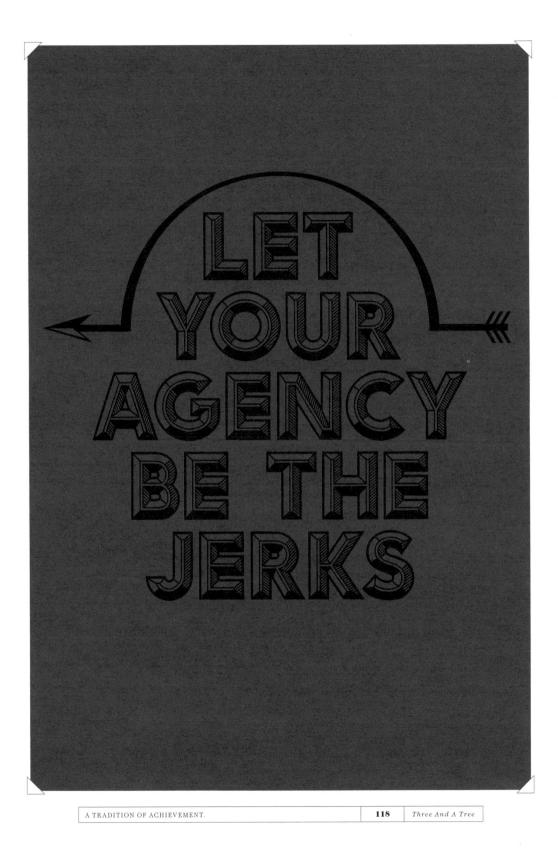

We often hear things like "I've been recommending this for years, but nobody will listen." What's fascinating, though, is when we come in and make the exact same recommendations, suddenly the powers that be are all ears. It's amazing how, once you're writing a check to an outside consultant, their opinions are treated as gospel.

If you have trouble getting your opinion heard, see if your agency shares your view, then bring it in front of the opposing forces. A good firm will have no qualms with being the bad guys and telling an organization what it needs to hear. The worst it can mean is someone going against the recommendations of "outsiders," but in any case you'll still be the hero for bringing in the "experts."

A member of internal design staff at a long-standing client, upon being introduced to us, called us the "second wife," the woman brought in when the husband got tired of his tried-and-true spouse. It shocked us at the time, but the sentiment is understandable. Internal marketing staff is often looked at as "makers," as in, "can you make this for me by Friday." Suddenly, a hot shot branding firm is brought in to make everything better, and the internal marketing staff begins to circle the wagons. "I wish we had their budget," "I guess I can start cleaning out my office," and "what makes them think they know this place better than me. I've been here for 15 years" are just some of the things we've overheard.

Let's put a few of these concerns to rest. First, agencies are not coming in to take your job. It's much easier (and more cost-efficient) to fire an expensive marketing firm than it is to lay off valuable, loyal internal staff. Secondly, there's job security in the fact that agencies are far too costly to create everything that a school needs to run, not to mention difficult to manage (agencies are opinionated outsiders, remember). Finally, take comfort in that it's the responsibility of a good branding firm to help make sure you have all the tools you need to effectively communicate, and are the most well-versed in the brand internally, making you the go-to authority on all things brand related from now to infinity. They'll even help you get bigger budgets if they can prove success.

IF YOUR STAFF DOESN'T GET IT.

NOBODY WILL.

───────◎───────

As stated earlier in this book, a brand is a story, and like a good joke, it's all in the telling.

Every interaction someone has with your organization is an opportunity to shape your brand's perception. Can an adjunct professor explain your university's positive differentiators to someone at a conference? Does the person who answers the phone in financial aid know what "liberal arts" means? Do current students know what articles you're covering in your alumni magazine?

Companies with successful brands don't get there by keeping them a secret. They regularly communicate with their employees about changes within the company, what they mean, and how they'll move forward. But that's not always the case in higher education. Too often, a university's mission and goals are hidden in dry documents that get filed away in some Indiana Jones-style warehouse alongside the Ark of the Covenant and the bones of Jimmy Hoffa.

You've put a lot of time, money, and effort around the new brand. Tell people what it's all about, and they'll tell others for you.

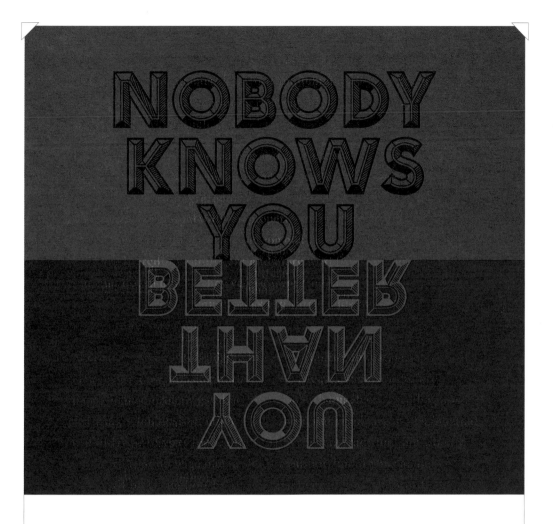

Faculty may not be the best marketers, but nobody knows their department or program better than they do. Find ways to incorporate their knowledge into your marketing materials. The anecdotes they can tell you about student interaction and success are often the best proof of the brand in action.

3

WHERE IT ALL GOES

TERRIBLY, LOPSIDEDLY, PEAR-SHAPED WRONG:

CREATIVITY

It was the great Woody Allen who said...

"Ninety percent of perspiration is just showing up." Or maybe it was George Carlin or Walt Twain or something. Either way, the time is going to come when everyone at your university finally gets tired of talking about branding, and a core group of people finally get together to do something. Huzzah: here comes the fun part.

Unfortunately, this is where it can all go terribly, horribly, lopsidedly pear-shaped and wrong. How? If you look toward other university work for inspiration. (Trust us, it's not there). If you think all your problems will be solved by a new logo or high-profile ad campaign (They won't, in fact, you'll create more). If your sole conceptual motif revolves around testimonials. If you rely on more of the same to get your new point across. If you fail to drag your institution out of the tired thinking that clichés like Three And A Tree are what's going to set your school apart.

A talented agency can help steer you away from clichés, but there will come a time when you'll need to create work on your own. This section of the book will help you kill the clichés, and stand on your own two feet, once and for all.

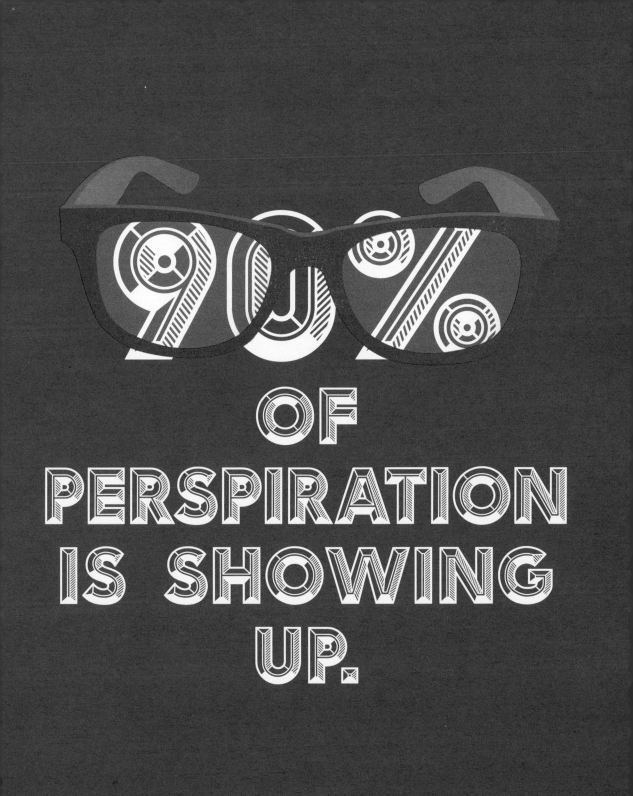

90% OF PERSPIRATION IS SHOWING UP.

(HEADLINE

––––––⊚––––––

Every effective marketing effort of the past century was created by a team of copywriters, art directors, and graphic designers. And most schools have at least one graphic designer on staff—but very few employ a marketing-centric copywriter. Maybe it's why, with very few exceptions, the vast majority of higher ed marketing is as dull as dirt.

A perfectly crafted headline will grab the attention of someone who doesn't want to read anything, and compel them to drop down to the smaller print. Great copy will keep them reading, and can deliver powerful messages that stick with people long after they've moved on.

Copywriting at the higher ed level usually falls to someone in the publications department, or the work-study student with a copy of Strunk and White. If headlines like "academic opportunity" and "student life" are the best you can muster, please hire a bona fide, honest-to-goodness copywriter.

GOES HERE)

Quick, besides your own, recite your favorite university tagline. Can't name any? Congratulations, you've arrived at the point of this spread. The reason "Just Do It," "I'm Lovin' It," and "The Ultimate Driving Machine" stick with you is because the companies marketing them are spending billions of dollars to back them up. No university tagline has ever had any lasting meaning for any of their intended audiences, yet schools still insist on them—and waste a lot of good money on their creation and implementation. If you MUST have a tagline, let us save you the effort. Select a three-word tagline from the list on the next spread, or make a fun game of it by flipping this book to a random page and using the line at the bottom of the page. (Now you know why those are down there!) Congratulations on your new university brand.

WE CAN'T MAKE THIS STUFF UP:

THE TAGLINES FEATURED AT THE BOTTOMS OF THE PAGES THROUGHOUT THIS BOOK HAVE BEEN DEVELOPED BY ACTUAL SCHOOLS!

WHY WE'VE NEVER CHANGED A LOGO

You got us. The simple answer: We don't want to fail. It's not that we can't craft logos. We do it all the time for our consumer clients, but universities are a completely different beast. A nasty one with several rows of teeth. Here's how the general scenario of higher ed logo design typically plays out:

--- 1 ---

Everyone doesn't think your current design is anything special, but they tolerate it, cause it's on a lot of buildings and business cards and such.

--- 2 ---

The new president decides it's time for a bold change, beginning with the logo.

--- 3 ---

A firm is hired.

--- 4 ---

Everyone, from students, to 80-year-old alumni, to the university mascot hates the new logo—even though the branding firm is only three days into the project and hasn't begun to sketch even the barest of ideas yet.

--- 5 ---

Someone writes a three-part exposé for the school paper detailing how much the design firm is being paid for the new logo—money that could go toward lowering tuition, new chairs for the dining hall, or puppies for all the sororities.

--- 6 ---

A Facebook group is started: "Outraged Students Against the New Logo." It gets 100,000 likes within 24 hours.

--- 7 ---

Via the school's legendary tunnel system that connects all the buildings together, the agency's designer is secreted to a bunker 10 stories below the provost's office. The designs are presented to a three person council, who immediately leak the designs to the school paper.

--- 8 ---

The football team's bus is overturned, and the marketing staff holes up in the bell tower with several days of simple provisions.

--- 9 ---

A modified version of the current logo is soon adopted, featuring a slight alteration to the logotype. The branding agency is never heard from again.

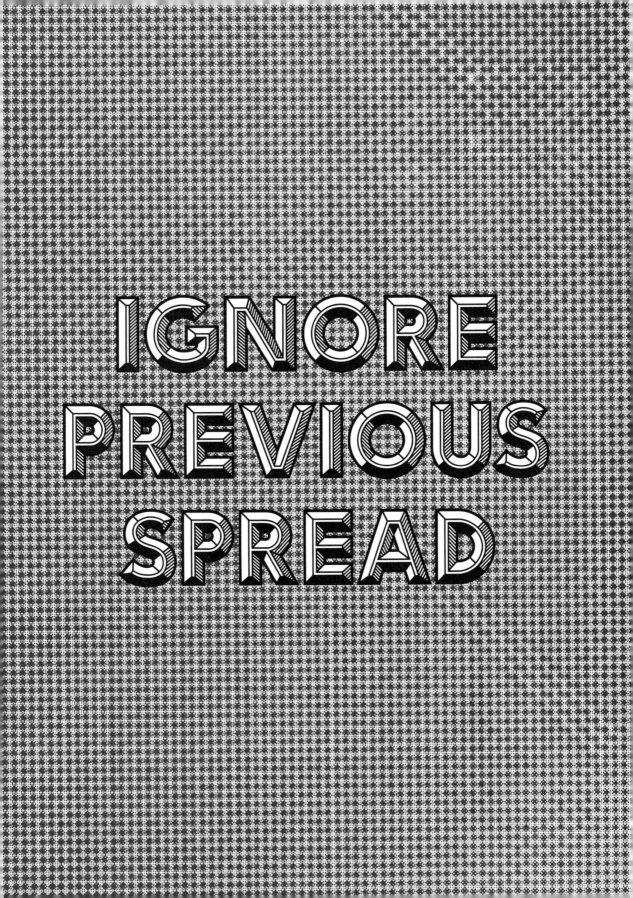

HOW TO MAKE A LOGO

At one time, every university had a seal. Then some wiseass decided universities needed logos, and now everyone has one.

If your logo does not feature at least one of the following icons, please adopt them immediately or risk having your accreditation revoked.

ABSTRACTION OF A PROMINENT UNIVERSITY DOME, TOWER, OR COLUMNED BUILDING	CROSS
	GRYPHON
OPEN BOOK	TORCH
LION	GENIE LAMP
SHIELD	YEAR OF YOUR FOUNDING

MILES. OF SMILES. AND MILES. AND MILES.

Man, do schools love advertising on billboards. On your next road trip with the family, try this fun car game: count the number of higher ed billboards featuring a giant, grinning head of a happy student, faculty member, or prominent alum. (Do donations of $100k and up come with a free billboard appearance?). Give yourself a bonus point for each billboard that includes the word "success."

For Wilkes University, we faced a unique dilemma. For several years, we worked hard to convey a brand that touted the personal attention students will find at Wilkes. When we had enough confidence in the brand to roll out an ad campaign, our media partner suggested billboards as the most efficient way to reach kids and parents. It's a big enough challenge to make people believe your school is a welcoming community of caring professors, it's even harder to do so on a 20' x 60' interstate billboard.

So what we created was essentially the anti-smiley billboard. If outdoor advertising is meant to reach the most people in the least intimate way possible, what if we did just the opposite? In small towns throughout our market, we created entire campaigns focusing on a single student from the local high school who we felt would fit in at Wilkes, kids who were good, solid, engaged students. We interviewed their friends and family to find out more about them, then crafted entire campaigns that spoke directly to them.

We started with billboards, but soon also began running the campaign in other outlets traditionally considered mass-media: television, mall kiosks, ads atop gas station pumps, transit advertising, and airplane banners. We found out where all the kids order their pizzas from on Friday nights, and dropped off limited-run pizza boxes to the shop owners. We even hid messages in fortune cookies at the local Chinese restaurants.

Lakeland senior

"Lauren McCabe"

You dream of becoming an accountant. Consider this Wilkes University's first major investment in you. Lauren, call a Colonel. 570.408.2023

Wyoming Area senior

"Paige Tronslen"

You help 2nd Graders prepare for their First Communion at St. Anthony's.

Wilkes University will help you prepare for many great firsts in your life. Paige, call a Colonel. 570.408.6032

Hazleton senior

"Alba Espizito"

As a future marketing specialist, you'll get people's attention. In fact, you've got all of Wilkes University's right now. Alba, call a Colonel. 570.408.6029

LAMAR

Holy Redeemer senior

"Josh Nintek"

As a math whiz, you can solve this problem:

If one Wilkes University freshman orders one large 16" pizza divided into 8 equal pieces, just how many of his 2,336 new friends will he be able to share it with? Josh, call a Colonel. 570.408.6027

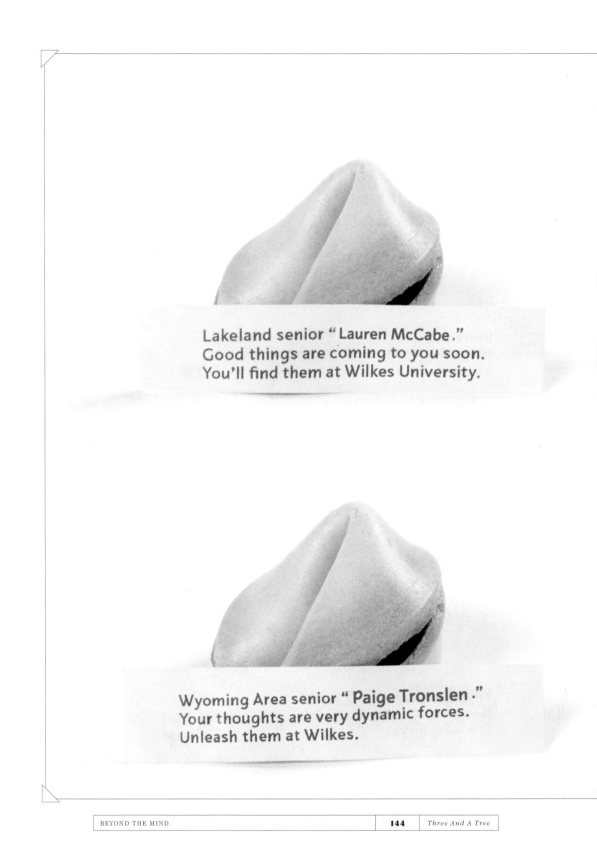

Lakeland senior "Lauren McCabe."
Good things are coming to you soon.
You'll find them at Wilkes University.

Wyoming Area senior " Paige Tronslen ."
Your thoughts are very dynamic forces.
Unleash them at Wilkes.

We initially got some criticism. Why would Wilkes waste all this money advertising to individual students, but they were kind of missing the point. If you were back in high school, and one day your town was blanked with ads from a university trying to recruit one of your class-mates, wouldn't you be talking about it in homeroom and at lunch. The high-school gossip mill got students talking about Wilkes in ways they never had before, and immediately boosted awareness of the previously little-known Wilkes. Not only that, the work was featured in every small-town newspaper where the campaign ran, more often than not on the front page. It was also picked up by *The New York Times*, *The Philadelphia Inquirer*, ABC News, FOX News, NPR, and MTV.

Ø

AND WE
NEVER HAD
TO RESORT TO
A SINGLE VAPIDLY
GRINNING MUG.

Ø

+ P.142-144 Wilkes University advertising campaign.

WHEN TALKING HEADS

We've never read an interesting student quote, but they're the bread and butter of academic recruitment. Maybe it's because student photos are an easy way to fill space, and a canned student quote about "exciting opportunities" means less work for the writer.

Likewise, the most overused motif in college viewbooks is the student profile. These profiles are rarely compelling, and should come with a disclaimer reading "results not typical." Like weight-loss ads, kids know that the people chosen for these profiles are hand-picked super achievers, and probably graduated in the late '90s.

Play Full Story

Stefanie Rinza: The Animal Rescuer
Added October 1, 2009

STOP MAKING SENSE.

If you're going to feature a student quote or profile, make sure it's extraordinary. Every person has an interesting story to tell, but it takes a great storyteller (i.e., writer) to bring it to life.

Throughout 2009, *The New York Times* ran "One in 8 Million," a beautifully edited online series of audio interviews and photography capturing the stories of seemingly average New Yorkers. The profiles were stunning in their simplicity, and perfectly showcased how even the most seemingly mundane story can be brought to life.

+ ABOVE Stills from the "One in 8 Million" website.

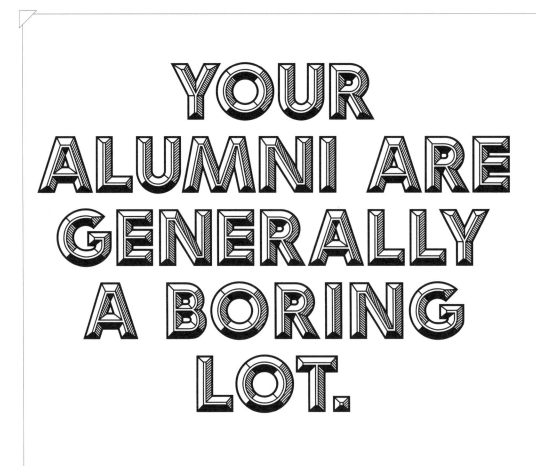

YOUR ALUMNI ARE GENERALLY A BORING LOT.

How many times have you read the opening to this article in a university magazine?

"When Bernard Jenkins ('63) graduated, he never dreamed he'd one day be (conducting medical research/leading a prominent LA dance troupe/a faceless Wall Street cog who just donated a million dollars to a new student center)."

Your alumni magazine is your most important and widely read piece of university communications, and should serve one purpose and one purpose only: engage readers with content that reflects the philosophy and values of the institution. There's a reason why most alums flip right to the class notes in the back of the mag: the rest of the magazine is dead boring. The problem is content: too many alumni mags rely on alumni profiles that are only of interest to the person being profiled and their roommate from 45 years ago.

Instead of focusing on people, look for the real story behind the person. When called upon to help the University of Dayton redesign its magazine, we saw the need for an editorial realignment. Our first issue included three features: one on an African village on the verge of extinction, another on the very real threat posed on governments by cyberterrorists, and the third an examination of political satire during the 2008 presidential election, featuring commentary from the graphic designer of John Stewart's "America: The Book." All three happened to include Dayton alums, but they were not the focus of the piece—the stories were. As a result, the stories (one of which was written by a freelance journalist hired specifically for the task) would have been at home in *National Geographic*, *Wired*, or *the New Yorker*, and the feedback we got from readers suggested they were actually read for once.

Kerry Temple, the editor of Notre Dame's magazine, has been publishing great content for years, which is why they're able to ask for—and receive—tens of thousands in voluntary subscriptions from readers who get the magazine for free regardless of their financial commitment.

Every school struggles with connecting in a meaningful way with their alums. If you're looking for a good place to start, invest in your alumni mag. Done right, it's an evergreen case statement for your institution.

LEAVE THOSE KIDS ALONE.

OR AT LEAST STOP SCARING THEM.

A few years ago, schools began to realize that they could get out in front of the game by sending mailers to high-school juniors and even sophomores (and probably by now, freshmen), before the tidal wave of materials hits students' mailboxes their senior year. Problem is, many schools have failed to account for the fact that these kids are more likely to be focused on awkward outgrowths of facial hair and getting gum stuck in their retainer than on choosing a college. So maybe a postcard series boasting of your new polymer centrifuge and prospects' future ability to conduct interdisciplinary lab work as early as their first semester is a little premature.

For Loyola University Maryland, we created a four-part junior search piece that took the focus completely off the university and instead sympathized with the fact that high school kids are under constant pressure to make big decisions earlier and earlier in life. The first piece (printed on tabloid-sized newsprint) encouraged kids to breathe a little—to experiment, and find out what they enjoy out there in the big wide world. The second piece continues the conversation, and only very lightly showcases Loyola as a place where you can continue this exploration—a very pure interpretation of our brand for Loyola as a place that helps students become "infinitely adaptable" for whatever they face in life.

In whatever you do, consider the person you're talking to. They're not a target audience. They're your daughter, brother, father, cousin, neighbor, or friend. Consider where they are in life, and talk to them in tones they can relate to.

Show me a 17-year-old who can properly define "liberal arts" or "research institution," and I'll show you the son of a provost or director of research. Kids are incredibly intelligent and more worldly than you might think. But that doesn't mean they've been working in an admissions office for the past 15 years or can discuss the intricacies of various classroom instructional methods.

There's a classic bit of advice in the marketing industry: "show, don't tell." Kids have never purchased a college education before. Their parents have probably only done it once themselves, and that was 25 years ago. Don't assume they understand higher ed jargon. It's fine that you're proud of your long-standing liberal arts tradition, but when you lead with that on page one, a significant portion of your audience may very well be turned off by the very appearance of the word "liberal." Instead of relying on insider language or trite phrases like "global" and "hands-on," explain your school's philosophy in a way that can be universally understood. And your message becomes clearer when you can offer concrete, compelling examples of that philosophy at work.

JUST BECAUSE SOMEONE CAN TAKE A PICTURE DOES NOT MAKE THEM A PHOTOGRAPHER.

Universities market themselves in hundreds of ways, and there's always a need for as many great photographs as possible. Spend money on a quality photographer, and you'll have a bank of valuable assets you can use for years.

If you're in a region that goes through noticeable seasons, you may have only two windows a year when kids are on campus and the weather/landscaping is ideal—in early May, and mid-September to early October, which also seem to always be the most rain-prone times of the year. Plan well in advance, especially when establishing annual budgets, and supply your photographer with a detailed list of photographs you hope to obtain. Allow them time for a day of scouting—or two if you have a massive campus—and make sure you build in time for weather-related delays (and obtaining weather-related production insurance isn't a bad idea either). Arrange for transportation during the shoot. A golf cart is ideal. And don't be afraid to hire an excellent photographer with limited higher-ed work in her portfolio. You're likely to get an unexpected style that stands out in the marketplace.

Schools love to feature shots of kids using laptops. Be careful. You can easily have a viewbook full of kids with their heads buried in computers. And technology styles are quickly outdated, and you don't want to be the school that seems to still be using bondi blue iBook clamshells.

Schools often fall over themselves making sure EVERY kid in EVERY photo is wearing some sort of Uni-branded merchandise, making the viewbook appear to be the glossy, well-produced manifesto of a shambling, hoodied cult, or at the very least, a merchandise catalog for your bookstore. If you're not photographing your students candidly (ideal), ask them to dress in comfortable everyday clothing, and bring a few backups that are actually in their wardrobe. That way you'll have options for the girl who wants to create an impression by coming dressed up in her ball gown (true story) or the guy who wants the world to know his position on the Second Amendment via his T-shirt (also true). You want potential students to be able to see themselves in your student body. Your kids may truly love your school, but the hoodie uniform masks the individual style of your students and makes you look like another generic school with a boxload of Champion sweatshirts.

→

ALL KILLER

→

NO FILLER

+ P.161-163 A selection of interior spreads from 160over90 higher education publication designs.

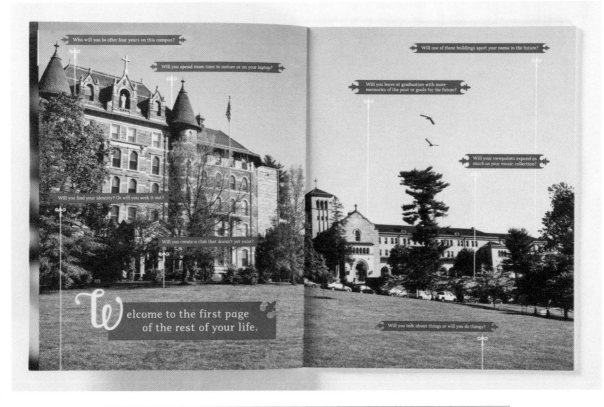

SPARTANS HAVE BEEN KNOWN TO GO THE EXTRA MILE. SOMETIMES THEY GO THE EXTRA 7,953 MILES

ANTHONY ARRIVED AT WILKES A GROUNDED INDIVIDUAL. WE HELPED HIM GET HIS HEAD IN THE CLOUDS.

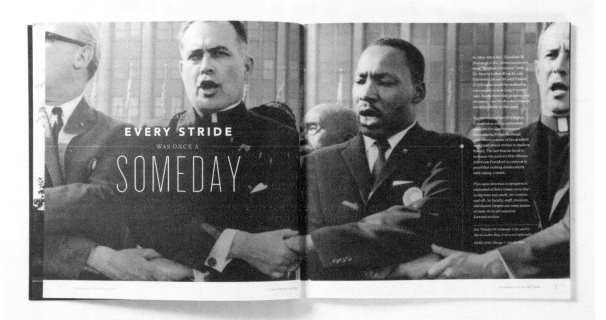

EVERY STRIDE
WAS ONCE A
SOMEDAY

LIVE ON A
SPRAWLING
259-ACRE ESTATE
AND STILL BE CLOSE
TO YOUR NEIGHBORS.

Walking through the University's campus, you're not the only one who feels right at home: approximately 90 percent of our undergraduates live in residence halls or the student neighborhood. Campus isn't just where you go to class. It's also where you learn to live on your own, make lifelong friends, play intramurals and organize activities.

First-year students live in Founders Hall, Marianist Hall, Marycrest Complex or Stuart Complex. Each of them is a community in itself, complete with a live-in staff and a student resident assistant on each floor, as well as study rooms, on-site copy machines, laundry facilities and a chapel. Don't forget your soda and surge protectors either. In every room, you'll find a small refrigerator and high-speed wireless Internet / cable TV / phone connections.

After your first year, you might move into spacious apartments or suites in the student neighborhood or into one of the comfortable houses where you can leisurely pass time on front porches. You'll appreciate your new home almost as much as the lush greenery and inspiring architecture. Our 259-acre campus was named one of the most significant campus sites in the country by the American Society of Landscape Architects. Beauty is all around you, not to mention just about everything else you need.

Where you live and you learn, from exams to Xboxes.

At UD, we realize that not everything you learn will come from the inside of a classroom or even a book (fact from it, in fact). That's why the University created Learning-Living Communities, or LLCs for short. Not only will your LLC immerse you in true collaborative learning with a group of your classmates, but it will also take you out of the classroom and into the world.

Here's how it works. All entering first-year students at the University take up residence in a Learning-Living Community. LLCs are hosted by a wide variety of interests. All LLCs participate in co-curricular events, too, from special guest lectures and film screenings, to field trips, service-learning projects, charity events and barbecues. Your LLC could be where your hallmates become your cinemates (not to mention your close friends), giving you a tight-knit group to study with, discuss issues and get advice from and even challenge to all-night, cut-throat Wii tournaments.

DON'T WE

For many schools, the opportunity to air a television ad is a rare opportunity. Television commercials are expensive to produce, and it's beyond the meager limits of most marketing budgets to allow for the frequency required to actually be effective (i.e., memorable) in the marketplace. That's why about the only time to spot a school's commercial is during the free airtime allotted by a network to both teams during halftime of a football game—if the school is lucky enough to have a football team good enough to have its games televised.

Maybe that's why a lot of schools fumble these opportunities. When it comes to commercials, a lot of university presidents want a pair of chinos. A little formal, but casual enough to wear to the tailgate. And durable. Just a simple montage of campus shots interspersed with clips of a professor at a blackboard, a solo violinist on-stage at the art center, and a researcher mixing some test tubes. A voiceover reading a mission statement over a backing track of the band performing the fight song. Let's not put on something distinctive that could possibly upset the bosses (the board of trustees, and alums).

R CHINOS.

Problem is, you don't get noticed in chinos.

The goal for a university television spot is not to outdo other university spots. On TV, the bar for higher ed commercials is extremely low—but they're not your competition. Mercedes-Benz, Budweiser, and ESPN are. On TV, you're playing against the big boys, with budgets 20x your size, while you're working with production dollars on the level with the local Tri-state Kia dealer. Avoid the temptation to try and get 15 shots of your campus, a pan-up of the bell tower, your mascot, and your entire sophomore class into 30 seconds. Your best approach is to develop a concept that is simple, smart, and communicates a single idea, ideally a message that delivers on your Unique Selling Proposition. They're the commercials that can be heard among all the other noise on TV, and maybe, just maybe, can get someone to pause long enough while fast-forwarding on the DVR to take notice.

YOUR TOUR IS YOUR BRAND

ALL OVER CAMPUS.

You've got an admissions director you'd trust with your life savings, or at least your endowment, at a Vegas baccarat table. Your mail house is stocked and ready to roll with tens of thousands of copies of your $10-a-pop viewbook. Your admissions staff is burning $4-a-gallon gas criss-crossing the region to spread your message to high schools. The website you spent seven figures on is doing its job of getting kids to schedule a campus visit. Your lobby is filled six days a week with nervous kids and their parents looking for evidence that you deserve their $100,000 investment—likely to be the second-most expensive purchase of their lives. And now their entire decision could very well lie in the hands of a junior communications major with two hours of training and a habit of looking at his shoes when he talks to people.

Whenever we visit a school for the first time, we take a campus tour, and we've witnessed some real stunners, like the one that began in the dank basement cafeteria with the boarded-up windows, or the one where our guide advised everyone (including the shocked parents) on which dorm was easiest to sneak beer into. Then there was the one that included an extensive walk through the trash-strewn parking lot adjoining the cemetery, giving us plenty of time to contemplate our own mortality.

It never ceases to amaze how much schools will spend per-student on recruitment, then treat the campus tour—the test drive, the open house, and the final sales pitch all wrapped into one—as an afterthought. You already know that if you can get a student to take a tour, he or she is much more likely to apply. But what if you treated the tour as if it was your ONLY chance to talk to that prospective student. Because in many cases, it may very well be just that.

Spend the money to hire a tour consultant and make recommendations. Then actually follow up on those recommendations to make the event memorable and fun. Invest in making your admissions lobby the most beautiful place on your campus. Beg your best faculty to get involved. Whatever it takes.

Better yet, why not consider hiring professional tour guides—like the amazingly engaging and often-entertaining guides you'll find at even the dullest historical sites. We're not aware of any school that's actually taken this leap, but for an interaction as important as this, why wouldn't you?

The people who enroll in colleges, donate to universities, matriculate to medical school, award research grants, tailgate at football games, and accept teaching positions are not target audiences. They're your children, brothers, aunts, neighbors, and friends. They read *Cosmopolitan*, *The Economist*, *ESPN The Magazine*, and *Wired*, Steven King novels and Malcom Gladwell essays. They drive Minis, Priuses, Ford F-150s, Harley-Davidsons, and John Deeres. They drink Tazo tea, Mountain Dew, Vitamin Water, tap water, and Chimay, eat at Pei Wei, Panera, and In-n-Out. They watch the Daily Show, Glenn Beck, Mad Men, Life With Jim, True Blood, and Curb Your Enthusiasm. They shop at Ikea, Wal-Mart, Target, and Piggly Wiggly. They blog, tweet, post, download apps, upload videos, Farm their Ville, and update their status.

So where do most higher ed marketers turn to for inspiration when it comes to university marketing materials? Other higher ed marketing materials, it seems.

You are not 17. And potential students aren't 45. Know your audience.

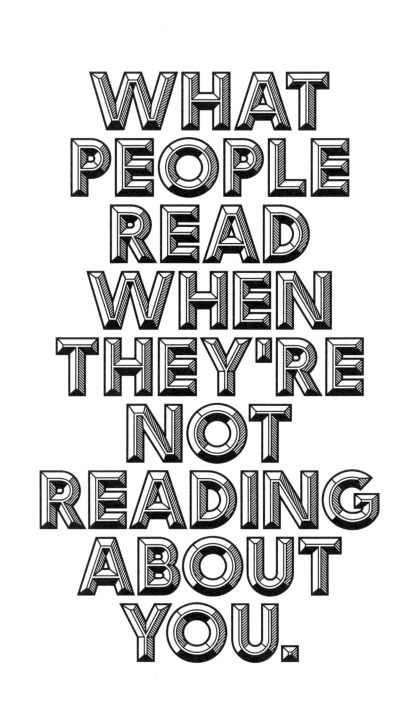

WHAT PEOPLE READ WHEN THEY'RE NOT READING ABOUT YOU.

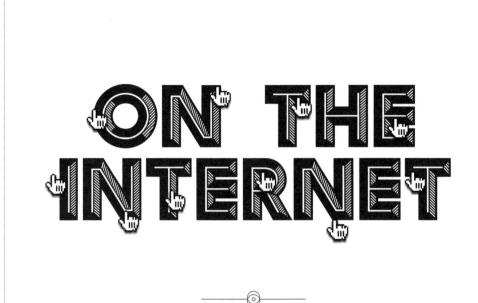

ON THE INTERNET

Here's the situation we typically find ourselves up against in the early stages of a brand relaunch with a new higher ed client:

The university wants a new brand. Its website, however, was just redesigned in the previous year under the old brand. A huge committee was formed to see it through. The process was arduous and harrowing, and by the time of the launch, almost everyone involved was doing their best to distance themselves from the project. The site was launched months behind schedule, was overbudget, and nobody seems to be happy with the final result. Students complain to anyone who will listen about the confusing navigation. Faculty from far-flung corners of the school jockey to have their information pushed up to the home page. Those responsible for entering content complain about having to sit through countless hours of training and the clunkiness of the Content Management System. A rogue department develops its own site design, and pushes to have it implemented on its section of the site. Designers and programmers argue over implementation, neither refusing to give an inch.

Then a new agency comes along, and gets asked the inevitable question: We don't want to go through this again anytime in the near future. How can this site be integrated into the new brand?

It's for all these reasons why we used to shy away from university sites, because there just didn't seem to be any way to guarantee success. The seemingly insurmountable bureaucracy we would be up against assured us we'd be left holding the bag, and the resulting cloud over us would tarnish our reputation, putting the rest of our work with the school—and the brand—in serious jeopardy. Instead, we chose to work in areas where we had more of a chance of being successful, which was usually on an admissions-only microsite, where we could work with a manageable core group on a section of the site that would be seen by a lot of kids, but wouldn't be under the close scrutiny and criticism of the wider university community.

For a while, our plan worked, and we saw great success launching a number of admissions sites for clients. But more and more we found ourselves being asked to tackle sites for other departments, and finally, universities as a whole. We knew a bottom-up approach of tackling a site—retrofitting navigation and design from one section of a site to work with the thousand other pages in every corner of a school's site—was out of the question. So the first time we accepted a commission to eat the whole cow and design and build a site from the top down, we decided to set some rules for engagement. Those rules eventually became our Website Process, and we now refuse any project that doesn't allow us to work within this tightly defined system of working, as it's the only way we've found that offers the greatest chance of a successful relaunch.

BEGIN WITH

THE

END

IN MIND.

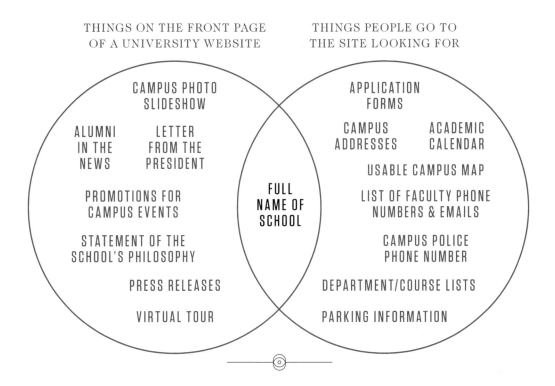

THINGS ON THE FRONT PAGE OF A UNIVERSITY WEBSITE

CAMPUS PHOTO SLIDESHOW

ALUMNI IN THE NEWS

LETTER FROM THE PRESIDENT

PROMOTIONS FOR CAMPUS EVENTS

STATEMENT OF THE SCHOOL'S PHILOSOPHY

PRESS RELEASES

VIRTUAL TOUR

FULL NAME OF SCHOOL

THINGS PEOPLE GO TO THE SITE LOOKING FOR

APPLICATION FORMS

CAMPUS ADDRESSES

ACADEMIC CALENDAR

USABLE CAMPUS MAP

LIST OF FACULTY PHONE NUMBERS & EMAILS

CAMPUS POLICE PHONE NUMBER

DEPARTMENT/COURSE LISTS

PARKING INFORMATION

In our opinion, the number one reason most college and university websites fail is in their attempt to become an information clearinghouse—a place to publish every possible bit and byte and detail on the school for any audience that could conceivably need to interact with a site. Every department and program needs their vitals listed. A public calendar needs to be listed. All university news, major and minor, must be featured on the home page. Food services has to post its daily menus. The library needs a main link to a searchable database of all its holdings. Then there are the sports scores, job openings, class schedules, faculty benefit information, international student pages, conference facility booking forms, student blogs, the President's page, alumni social networks, internal email portals, search bars, endless drop downs, site maps, etc., etc.

Pity the poor high school student who has to wade through all this—and a snow closing emergency notice front and center on the home page—in order to find out why he or she should be applying to your school in the first place.

INFOGRAPHIC SOURCE: THEDONUTPROJECT.COM

It's obvious that these attempts to become information clearinghouses quickly result in information overload. Consider this: In 2009, a survey for one of our clients found that more than 92 percent of prospective students used the school's website as their first and primary point of information before deciding to apply. And that number's not going to go down.

Schools simply aren't dedicating enough effort to making their .edu experiences relevant and meaningful for one of their most vital audiences—leading us to one of our core principles for higher ed web design: instead of being an information clearinghouse, schools should instead dedicate their .edu as a marketing-only site, offering only enough information to key audiences to allow them to make a decision on how they wish to engage with the school.

You heard us right.

A MARKETING-ONLY SITE.

It's a huge mindshift, but it works. Just look at the sites of any for-profit school for evidence.

The hinge there is what we define as "key audiences." Put simply, these are the audiences that represent the greatest source of revenue to a school, and aren't currently in a relationship with you. In other words, they're just interested in dating right now. For most schools, these are prospective undergrads and grads, prospective undergrad parents and guidance counselors, athletics visitors, potential faculty, and alumni. In some cases, this list could be expanded to include research resources, medical centers, or any other significant source of revenue.

But what of all the people who are currently engaged with the school? They write tuition checks. Isn't that a significant source of revenue? So where should we list course schedules and class information. And while we're at it, why can't we put the library on there too? And meal plans!

Don't do it. Don't. Take all that other stuff—the thousands of pages your already-engaged audiences visit on a regular basis—and sequester them off on a separate site. Maybe it's a subdomain, maybe it's available behind a login page. Or maybe it's an entirely different URL altogether. The message here is that if you don't bifurcate your site into a marketing-only site and an information-clearinghouse site, you will probably fail. Fail in the sense that your site will devolve into a befouled, muddled, cluttered mess. Just like every other university site.

Once you've cleared the decks for a marketing site, build a strategy. Nothing complicated, just a single 11x17 page where you list out the key audiences you defined above. Then list what you want from each audience. For potential undergrads, it's usually "learn more, visit the campus, or apply." For alumni, it's often "encourage engagement and donating." And so on and so forth.

Now comes the brutally fun part, where you list out the support points (and only the support points) that will encourage your audience to act in the way you want it to. Will your academic philosophy, your academic programs, and your student living options encourage a potential undergrad to visit or apply? Of course they will. Put 'em on the list. Will your meal plans do the same? Unless your cafeteria offers a nightly all-you-can-eat raw bar and a crab meat and flying fish roe risotto, we're sorry, VP of Dining Services, but your information belongs elsewhere. And so it goes all the way down the line, because unless it's information that moves your audience one step further toward making a decision, it's filler that's distracting them from your core message.

Once you're done, congratulations: you have the makings of a Web Strategy. A one-page document detailing exactly what should go on your marketing site. And another long list of stuff that'll go on your new site for already-engaged audiences. Once finalized, your Web Strategy document should become sacrosanct. It is the guiding hand that will allow you to construct a tightly focused sitemap, wireframe, design comps, and eventual website. But only if—and this is a big if—you don't diverge from this Strategy document one iota. Because at some point, maybe on the second round of wireframes, someone's going to say "you know, I was thinking. Wouldn't it be cool if..." Stop thinking. Look at the strategy. Is it on there? Will your new thing drive our audience to react in the way we hope? No? Then it dies, right here and now. Be ruthless. Be Dirty Harry. Any addition that diverges from the original plan, no matter how seemingly insignificant, can bring your interactive house of cards crashing down. If you've realized, however, that this is an oversight, stop all work immediately.

Let's say—as we did with one client—that a key audience was missed in the Strategy phase. As we were putting the final site through its paces, someone mentioned that parents of current students at this particular school actually donated in droves—above and beyond what they were already paying for tuition (amazing, right?). Yet there was no section of the site dedicated to them. Now we could have just tacked on a section and hoped our duct-tape solution took care of itself, but we instead went all the way back to the strategy phase. We considered parents, what motivated them to donate, and listed out what we'd like them to know. We then integrated this information into the sitemap, giving parents their own top-level navigation item. Wireframes were redrawn, new designs were comped, and the programmers went to work on building an easy form to facilitate donations. Because we went back to square one and let our strategy be our guide, we didn't bust six months of work to make a major addition. Had we done otherwise, our solution might have looked as slapdash as the other obvious add-ons that creep into most university sites just weeks into a launch.

Employed properly, your Web Strategy is your Bill of Rights, 10 Commandments, and Magna Carta all rolled into one. It should be visited anytime anyone's tempted to make a material change to your site, large or small, before any programmer or designer starts building stuff. People WILL get frustrated. This is the web, after all. It was designed to allow for quick additions of content.

A good test for the usability of your site is to count up all the links on your home page. We think you'll be surprised at the final number. Ask yourself what is the absolute minimum number of links possible, then work toward that number.

THE TECHNOLOGY TRAP

⊘

FLASH INTROS.
MESSAGE BOARDS.
ITUNESU.
PODCASTS.
YOUTUBE.
PROPRIETARY SOCIAL NETWORKS.
GOOGLE CALENDAR INTEGRATION.
CHAT ROOMS.
BLOGS.
DIGG LINKS.
RSS FEEDS.
FACEBOOK.
TWITTER.
FOURSQUARE.
INSTAGRAM.

⊘

Universities love to jump to the latest gewgaws and try to shoehorn them into every corner of the site ("hey, I bet kids will love Twittering their junior-year poly-sci curriculum"). We've seen schools dedicate a lot of time, money, and resources building far-flung technologies into their sites. Often with little payoff.

We once built an entire social network for accepted students. And it was really successful—it was even featured on the front page of the Business section of *USA Today*. That success lasted about 20 months—because we had essentially duplicated something that already existed and was beginning to get some significant momentum behind it: Facebook.

Before jumping into any technological rabbit hole, take a good, sober look at whether it's worth the investment. Should you build an entire password-protected network for your alumni, or should you take advantage of the network that's already waiting for you on Facebook? Do you really need a YouTube page if nobody's producing any engaging video content? How relevant will a Twitter feed on your homepage be if your faculty couldn't be bothered with posting anything?

When done well, social media can go a long, long way in furthering your messaging and building a fervent fan base. The key is in developing a content strategy that plans releases well in advance, and is parsed out in regular, effective air strikes. Does your school have a team that can be solely dedicated to maintaining your social media networks? If not, you're likely to hear crickets or spot some tumbleweeds after the initial enthusiasm fades and your audience has moved on to something else.

You can have a lot of expensive, shiny tools in your garage, but if they're not being put to good use, they're clutter. As time goes by, you'll probably forget why you bought them in the first place. And think of the opportunity cost of the things you could have been doing.

YOU'RE NOT SPENDING ENOUGH ON YOUR WEBSITE.

A survey for a client revealed that nine out of 10 potential freshmen did their initial research on the school's website.

The school spent $15,000 on a recent site relaunch.

Like the school, you're probably not allocating nearly as much as you should on your site. The web doesn't require printing, mailing, or media costs, but you should be investing at a rate that allows your site to be mind-blowing from that first point of contact. Beause they'll never get a chance to see your fancy 48-page, perfect bound, french-folded and embossed viewbook if they don't get past your lousy home page.

PATHWAYS TO GREATNESS

Why do schools save their dopiest themes for when they're trying to make the biggest impact—like when they're kicking off a $200 million Capital Campaign?

HOW TO KNOW WHEN
YOU'RE IN OVER YOUR HEAD.

One of the 160over90 creative directors worked with a particularly difficult university at a previous agency. After sharing a piece of direct mail with the President, he exclaimed "this is all wrong."

"What is?" asked the creative director.

"None of these students are looking up."

"Up?" the CD asked.

"Yes, up! They should all be looking up in the sky, like they're looking toward their future."

"Well, this piece has at least 10 photos in it. How many students should be looking up at the sky."

"All of them."

The next version of the direct mail piece portrayed a student body that looked like it was collectively witness to the Second Coming.

WHO'S PAYING FOR THAT NEW LIBRARY?

———⊚———

Kids don't care about that new $20 million building that will be completed two years after they graduate. In fact, they probably have a deep disdain for it, since it represents what their tuition will really be spent on. So hold off on the renderings in your viewbook. Save the space for photos once it's done.

KIDS
A
DON'T
BULLSHIT
READ
OVERGENERALIZATION.

Respect—don't underestimate—your audience. Kids will read if the copy is interesting, well-written, and relevant. If it's not, we don't blame them for skipping it. Like you, they have better things to do.

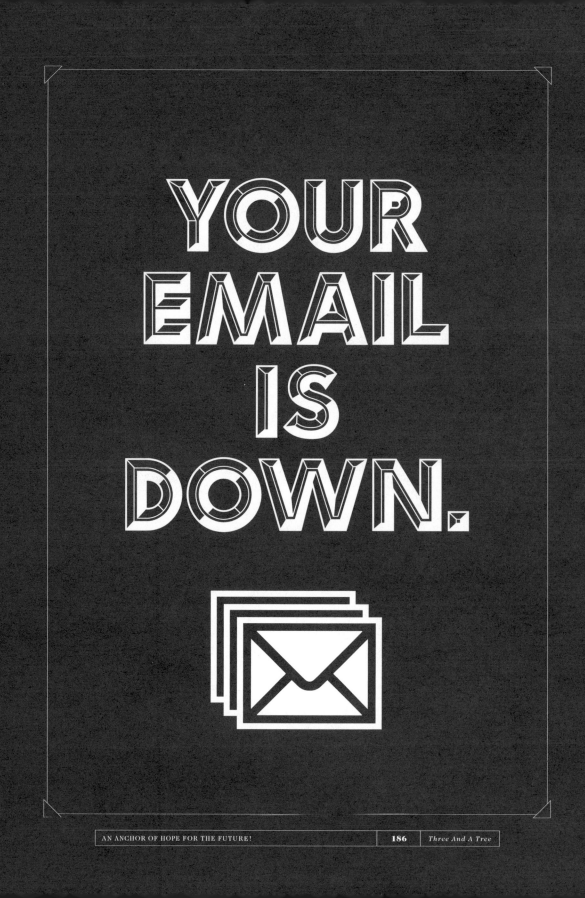

Reaching kids by email is cheap, but unlike their parents, most kids don't regularly check their email. In fact the percentage of kids who use email ages 12-17 drops every year. Crazy, right? Deal with it, and find better ways to talk to kids.

UD's DNA

Now you have a good feeling for what the University of Dayton is all about: challenging academics that ask you the tough questions, selfless service aimed at improving the world and, of course, having a blast with a tight-knit community that shares these same ideals. In addition, our tuition — $29,930/year (fall 2010) — makes the University of Dayton an excellent value among comparable private institutions.

As the largest private university in Ohio, we have many more qualities to consider. Some key facts and figures will give you a better idea of how high we stand compared to other institutions.

The People:

The people who populate the University of Dayton pride themselves on their openness, efforts to foster a friendly and warm community, and their commitment to engaging the world around them. With over 6,900 full-time undergraduates there is never a dull moment, and our over 900 full-time and part-time dedicated faculty will inspire and challenge you.

A BETTER WAY TO TALK TO KIDS.
EVENTUALLY

⊚

Ah...iPad strategies. Whenever we bring them up in a meeting with a client, people suddenly sit up straight and lean a little forward, like in those old E.F. Hutton commercials. Here's the skinny on iPads: At the time of this writing, about 9 percent of people accessing online university content are doing so on a mobile device—with about half of them using iPads.

Do you need to start figuring out how you're going to adapt your content for mobile devices like iPads and Android phones? Yes. Do you need to have it all wrapped up by next week? No. The vast majority of your audience is probably still using desktops and laptops to visit your web site. But the mobile audience is growing every day, and our research is showing it's an audience of highly qualified students and affluent alumni. If you want to reach this audience, you might want to consider getting on this sooner rather than later. That's why the University of Dayton asked us to deliver an interactive version of their viewbook as an iPad app—they see the potential, and they want to be first-to-market with innovations like this, instead of waiting until everyone else is on board.

+ P.188 University of Dayton iPad app.

THE RULE OF THIRDS

Once you count up the number of pages you think your site needs, challenge yourself to cut that number by 66 percent. Your users will thank you, as will your head of interactive.

HOW TO

WRITE
EDIT

SUCCESSFUL COPY FOR DIGITAL

Follow these simple steps when writing web copy:

──────────────── 1 ────────────────

GET EVERYTHING DOWN THAT YOU KNOW YOU WANT TO SAY.

──────────────── 2 ────────────────

EDIT UNTIL THE COPY IS TIGHT.

──────────────── 3 ────────────────

CUT IT IN HALF.

──────────────── 4 ────────────────

CUT IT IN HALF AGAIN.

──────────────── 5 ────────────────

DONE!

Any time you're trying to deliver more than your core brand message, you're diverting attention. Every touchpoint should drive home your core message as often as possible.

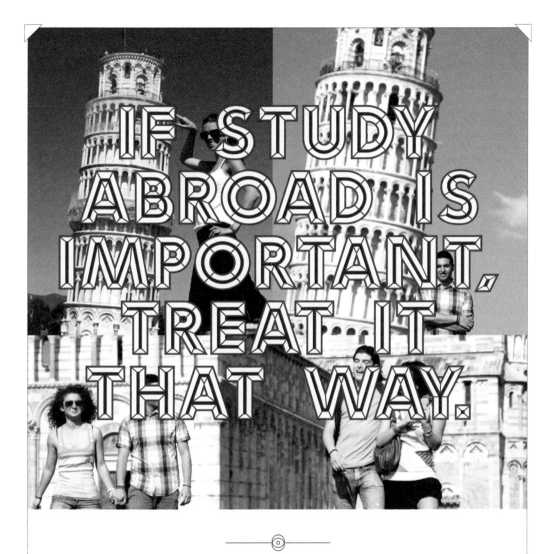

IF STUDY ABROAD IS IMPORTANT, TREAT IT THAT WAY.

Next to Three And A Tree, the second most cliché photo motif is the ill-lit, poorly composed snapshots of four female study-abroad students front of the Colosseum (or Parliament, the Eiffel Tower, etc.). Find another way to showcase study abroad.

Next on the list is the professor and student looking intently at a beaker.

SHOW THEM
—
DON'T TELL THEM

HOW YOUR SCHOOL OFFERS A
BETTER EDUCATION, AND YOU'LL
FIND THAT YOUR MESSAGE WILL
DO A MUCH BETTER JOB OF
STRIKING A CHORD.

DON'T RAP. EVER.

Your marketing should never feature anyone rapping.
Period. It's not cute, it's awkward, and it makes us all
a little uncomfortable to be around you.

REMEMBER THE ENVELOPE. PLEASE.

Higher ed marketers spend days agonizing over the cover of a brochure, but if the envelope it's being mailed in isn't at least as compelling as the cover, they've failed.

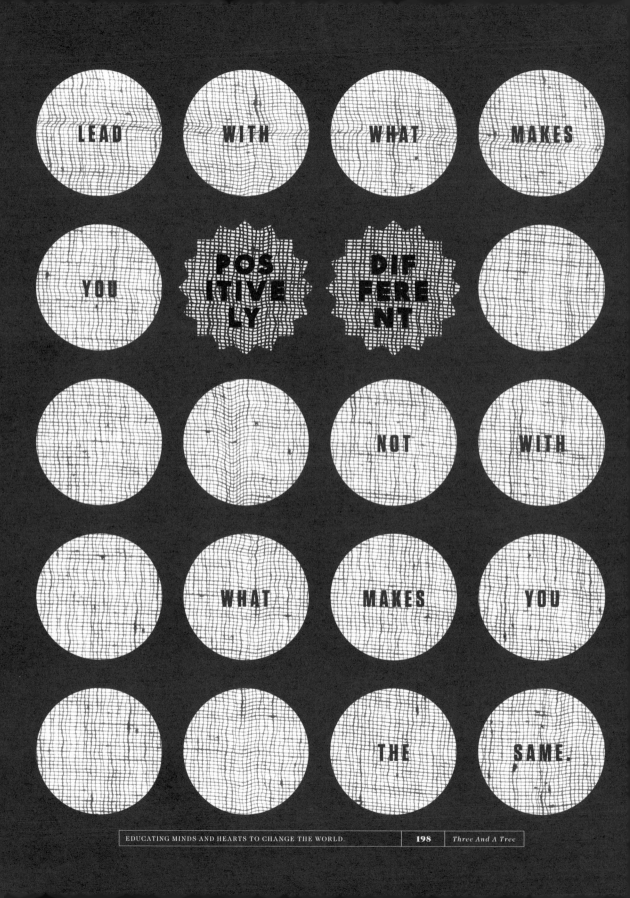

Any graduate ad featuring the words "convenient evening and weekend classes" somewhere in the copy is ineffective, because that's the exact same benefit every other graduate program in the country is leading with. You don't have the time or money to bring someone around to consider graduate school, but you can convince those who aren't on the fence to choose your graduate school—if you can tell them why you'll offer the best experience beyond offering Thursday night classes and a building just off the interstate.

OUR
COMMENCEMENT
SPEECH

This book isn't complete. Hell, it may leave you with even more questions. We had to keep some secrets back from our competitors who are reading this (and no doubt shouting "bullshit!" at every other page). As this book goes to press, we're continuing to learn, and constantly making mistakes.

Please don't hesitate to reach us with any thoughts, comments, or questions you may have. You can reach us at contact@160over90.com

For more insights into the mysterious people behind this book, visit 160over90.com, read our blog at 160over90.com/blog, and follow us on Twitter: @160over90.

And good luck with your brand. No higher ed brand rollout is without its flaws, but hopefully you were able to glean a few nuggets of insight to set you on the right path.

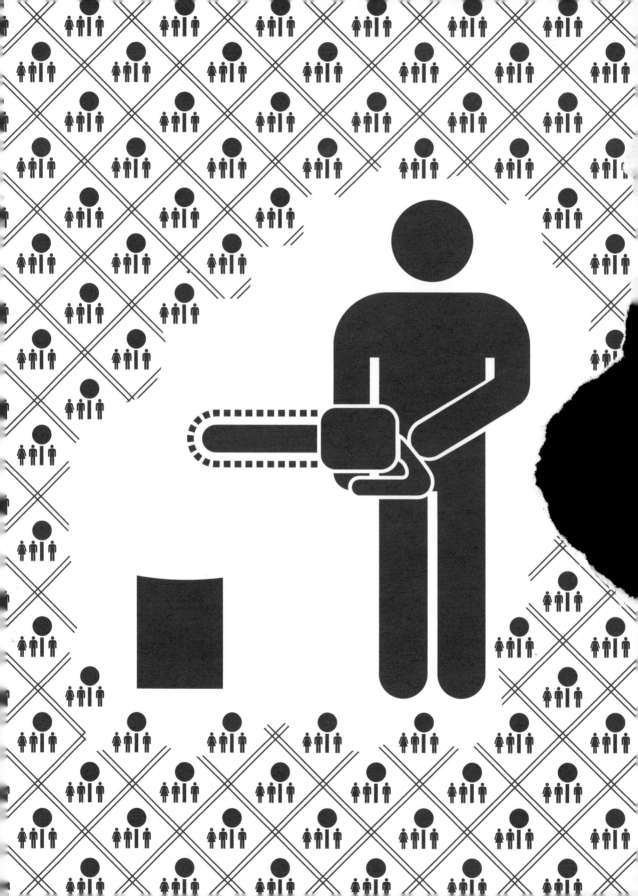